level one
JOURNEY
GROUPS

A Relational Discipleship Experience

Primary Scriptures Versions used in this work are ESV and NIV unless otherwise noted.

The Holy Bible, English Standard Version. ESV® Text Edition: 2016. Copyright © 2001 by Crossway Bibles, a publishing ministry of Good News Publishers.

Holy Bible, New International Version®, NIV® Copyright ©1973, 1978, 1984, 2011 by Biblica, Inc.® Used by permission. All rights reserved worldwide.

Published by Deeper Walk International.

First Edition February, 2021 / Printed first in the United States of America

ISBN: 978-1-7327510-6-4

Deeper Walk International
13295 Illinois St. #223
Carmel, IN 46032

www.DeeperWalkInternational.org

level one
JOURNEY
GROUPS

A Relational Discipleship Experience

AMY HAMILTON BROWN

CONTENTS

UNIT 5: GOD'S HEART & MY HEART

UNIT 6: HEALING HEARTS

APPENDICES

JOURNEY GROUPS

Welcome to Journey Groups, and to a unique relational discipleship experience! Over our first four years, we've seen hundreds of people experience transformation through their participation in Journey Groups, so we invite you to join us in using our particular methods of facilitation.

We designed Journey Groups to be relationally driven and content rich. Although our content is excellent, it will only bring about deep transformation when experienced in relationship. You can read this book and learn some wonderful concepts, and you are welcome to do that. We strongly recommend, however, that you take one of two paths:

1. join an online or local Journey Group led by one of our certified leaders,[1] or

2. invite some friends to join you, follow our facilitation methods, and experience relational discipleship!

FACILITATOR'S GUIDE

If you'd like to join the community of people around the world who are growing together in these concepts and learning how to facilitate transformational groups, please investigate the Deeper Walk Certified Journey Group Leadership Community at the link in the footnote below.[2] The fellowship is warm, the training is excellent, and there are many benefits to being part of our Community!

Another excellent resource to prepare you to lead a group is the Deeper Walk International E-Institute Course, "Journey Groups: An Introduction to Relational Discipleship."[3] This course features author and Journey Group Director Amy Brown and experienced Journey Group Leaders as they walk through our facilitation methods and provide an overview of the content of each unit.

Our first unit, Jumpstart, outlines the key components of a Journey Group meeting. The components of Check In, Appreciation, and Listening to Jesus are essential to the Journey Group experience, and you'll find in-depth information about these components in the Jumpstart unit. Another essential component to include in your Journey Group is COCOA, the acrostic for our Guidelines. COCOA is explained in Jumpstart, Lesson 1. Please don't try to lead a Journey Group without these essential elements in place!

Journey Groups meetings are most effective if they last between one and two hours. This gives enough time for you to include all the essential compo-

---

1 | www.deeperwalkinternational.org/journey-group-directory

nents and for discussion of the lesson. We recommend that you begin and end at your scheduled time so that you are honoring the members' time.

Here is a suggested outline for a Journey Group meeting:

Welcome and Check In. We've found that approximately two minutes is a good guideline for each person's Check In. Encourage members to look at the Appendix "SASHET," which provides a list of emotion words. This is very helpful for members who aren't accustomed to naming their emotions.

Appreciation. If your meeting lasts one hour or if you have a large group, you may want to keep Appreciation Stories short. You might ask a question like, "What made you smile today?" If your meeting lasts longer or your group is very small, each person can share an Appreciation Story, including a brief description of what occurred, what they appreciated, and how they felt in their emotions and body. Again, we use the guideline of two minutes for a short Appreciation Story.

Discussion. It's important that members first share what God highlighted to them in the lesson, rather than the leader explaining concepts or stating what was most important. In Journey Groups, we are encouraging each person to develop their interactive relationship with God, and noticing what felt important or stood out to them is a helpful part of this process. Explanations of content are necessary only if your group members ask questions.

Listening to Jesus. This portion of the meeting is the most important element, and can be done in several ways. Often, we end our discussion about 20 minutes prior to the end of the meeting, and take 5-10 minutes to sit quietly, invite Jesus's presence, and notice what thoughts float through our minds. After this time, each member is invited to share what thoughts were helpful or brought them peace. Because learning to quiet our minds is a key step to hearing God's voice, we encourage members that simply sitting quietly during this time is a success. This is a gentle time of listening for ourselves rather than looking for advice for others.

During the Listening to Jesus portion of the meeting, you may occasionally lead the group to invite God's thoughts about a particular topic. Because we want to develop our skill at noticing what God might be impressing on us individually, we use guided listening only occasionally.

Whatever form we use for listening, we invite members to share the thoughts that gave them peace. We also allow members to "pass" on sharing any time they prefer to do that.

We are very excited that you are reading this book and interested in relational discipleship through Journey Groups! Thank you for joining us, and may you find joy in the journey.

Amy Hamilton Brown and

Deeper Walk International Journey Group Leaders

jumpstart
UNIT ONE

jumpstart
LESSON 1

Foundations

Welcome to Jumpstart! Over the next four weeks, you'll taste a sampler of the life-changing materials we experience together in Journey Groups. In this lesson, we will talk about our guidelines, the concepts behind the way we meet, and the structure of our meetings.

GUIDELINES FOR OUR MEETINGS:

Our Journey Group Guidelines are designed to build community and ensure that we all feel welcome, safe, heard, and connected. Journey Group Guidelines use the acrostic "COCOA."

In Journey Groups, what we share is

Confidential; we

Observe time; we share as we are

Comfortable; we avoid

Overwhelm; and we skip the

Advice.

A little more about our guidelines:

1. What is shared in Journey Groups is confidential to the group and is not to be shared outside the group without the sharer's permission.

2. We try to keep our sharing to about two minutes per person per question so that everyone has an opportunity to add their thoughts. Your Journey Group leader will gently let you know if you *consistently* exceed this time.

3. Our goal in Journey Groups is to give each person the freedom to share at *their* comfort level. Some people feel comfortable sharing on a personal level quickly, while others prefer to keep their answers less personal or in-depth.

4. Recognizing overwhelm in ourselves and others is a skill we will gain in Journey Groups. We can overwhelm ourselves and our group members if we use too much intensity in our sharing, so this is another area where our leaders can gently guide us as we learn the skill.

5. In Journey Groups, we are learning to walk together while honoring God's individual guidance, so we offer encouragement to each other without advice.

CHECKING IN

We will begin each Journey Group meeting by Checking In.[1] What is Checking In? We check in by choosing one or two emotion words that describe our current feelings, and briefly describe what led to those emotions. S.A.S.H.E.T. (Sad, Angry, Scared, Happy, Excited, Tender)[2] is a simple acrostic of emotion words that you might want to use if you are not in the habit of noticing and sharing your emotions. However, you may check in with any emotion word that fits. Here's an example of Checking In:

> "Today I'm checking in as peaceful but sad. My daughter and I are especially close, and we have lots of fun together. She's been home for the last week. I'm sad because she went back to college today and I miss her, but I'm peaceful because I spent time with Jesus processing my sadness. I'm in."

We end our Check In with the phrase "I'm in" to signify we are finished checking in, but also that we are "all in" for group time together.

Checking In is a simple, relational practice which reminds us that our core goal is to express our glad-to-be-together joy in our relationships with each other and with God. In Journey Groups, we check in at the beginning of every meeting. Checking In is a way to identify and share where we are on the emotional map as we gather and is a time to turn from distractions and set our hearts to be fully present with the group.

DISCUSSING THE LESSON

You'll notice that when we discuss our weekly lesson, your Journey Group leader will ask a question like, "What did God highlight to you in this lesson?" or "What seemed important to you in this lesson?" In Journey Groups,

---

1 | Checking In originated with The LK10 Community at www.lk10.com in their Church 101 course.

2 | S.A.S.H.E.T. was developed by John White at lk10.com. In the appendices you will find an expanded list of S.A.S.H.E.T. words. We recommend that you keep a copy of it handy for your Journey Group meetings.

one goal is to stay connected to God and hear from Him on a regular basis. This means your leader won't identify for you the most important part of the lesson—God will highlight that to each of you as you read and discuss. God's way of highlighting important truth may look somewhat different for each of us—one person may notice and sense a concept or sentence is especially true, while another person might feel some excitement or great peace about a portion of the lesson. Most of us receive input from God but don't always recognize it because it can sound like our own thoughts. This is 100% okay—we ask you to notice what seems important to you, whether you had a sense of God communicating that to you or not.

APPRECIATION

The Word tells us to enter God's gates with thanksgiving (Psalm 100:4), and modern neuroscience has discovered that keeping our minds in a state of appreciation helps us stay connected to those we love (including God). In Journey Groups, we often add a time of sharing appreciation to our meetings in order to build joy, get to know each other, and grow our connections with each other and with God. We'll talk more about Appreciation in next week's lesson.

PONDER, JOURNAL, AND DISCUSS:

1. What stood out to you from this lesson? Be prepared to share that with your Journey Group when you meet.

2. Which of the Guidelines feels most helpful to you as an individual? Which feels most challenging? Is there one Guideline you would most like your Journey Group leader to consistently uphold?

3. We recommend that you begin a list of Appreciation Memories—specific memories of times when you felt joyful, peaceful, connected, and/or accepted. Try to add five memories to your list this week.

LESSON 2

Appreciation

Appreciation is packaged joy, and *joy means "someone's glad to be with me!"* When we remember and focus on the times in our life where we felt joyful, peaceful, accepted, and/or connected, we are training our brains to look for the good things in life.

An appreciation memory can range from small moments like a beautiful sunset or a friendly smile from a cashier to life-changing events like weddings or baptisms. It's not the size of the event that rewires our brains, it is the intentional focus on how it feels in our bodies and emotions to be joyful, peaceful, connected, or accepted.

Let's take a look at what Scripture says about appreciation (or thanksgiving), and compare it with what neuroscientists have learned about the brain in the last two decades:

"Let us come into his presence with thanksgiving." PSALM 95:2A

Appreciation activates the relational mind, which enables us to connect better with God and other people. We literally "come into His presence" when we are in a state of appreciation.

"I will give thanks to the LORD with my whole heart; I will recount all of your wonderful deeds." PSALM 9:1

When we focus on specific appreciation moments (every appreciation memory is a time when we experienced one of His deeds), our relational mind is activated, and we are better able to connect with Him.

"The LORD is my strength and my shield; in him my heart trusts, and I am helped; my heart exults, and with my song I give thanks to him." PSALM 28:7

When we are in a state of appreciation, we are better able to receive from God and others. He is always our strength and shield, but we can access His help more readily when we are feeling appreciative.

Notice the "glad to be together" joy and appreciation expressed in Psalm 100:

¹ Make a joyful noise to the LORD, all the earth!

² Serve the LORD with gladness!

Come into his presence with singing!

³ Know that the LORD, he is God!

It is he who made us, and we are his;

we are his people, and the sheep of his pasture.

⁴ Enter his gates with thanksgiving, and his courts with praise!

Give thanks to him; bless his name!

⁵ For the LORD is good;

his steadfast love endures forever, and his faithfulness to all generations.

We frequently share appreciation memories in Journey Groups because this turns our hearts and minds toward God, activates our relational brain, and enables us to sense His presence and His thoughts. You could say that appreciation is a gateway into God's presence, into His peace and love.

Since appreciation is such a powerful gift, we recommend that you begin collecting appreciation memories—specific memories when you felt joyful, peaceful, connected, or accepted. Some of these memories will include people, while others may be about times in nature, with animals, or in solitude. Some memories may bring high-energy joy to your mind, but appreciation memories may also be carriers of low-energy quiet and peace. Our minds function best in a rhythm between this high-energy joy and low-energy quiet, and appreciation is a tool that can help us establish that rhythm.

Begin your Appreciation Memory Library using the following tips:

- Specific memories work best to awaken your relational thinking, so it's more helpful to remember "breakfast with Jennifer when we talked about raccoons" than "I appreciate how much Jennifer loves animals."

- As you ponder or meditate on an appreciation memory, fully enter into it again; remember what you saw, heard, smelled, touched, and tasted, who was with you, the time of year, weather—any important details that help you really reconnect with the memory.

- When you are choosing a memory to help you get into relational mode, avoid memories that also have painful associations (or "splinters"). For instance, if you took a wonderful trip to the mountains with your friend who recently moved far away, this memory is likely to stir up feelings of pain along with appreciation. Splinter-free memories are best for stirring up appreciation.

- Keep a list or journal of your appreciation memories—something as simple as the Notes app on your phone, an index card, or a pocket-sized notebook. A short title of 2-3 words is sufficient; you'll find such a list is beneficial when you need a little boost to restore your sense of appreciation.

PONDER, JOURNAL, AND DISCUSS:

1. What stood out for you from this lesson? It might be something surprising, new, or something that strongly resonates for you. Be prepared to share this with your Journey Group.

2. As you are creating your Appreciation Memory Library, take time to notice how appreciation feels in your emotions and body. What are a few feeling or body sensation words you would use to describe how appreciation feels to you?

3. Text or call a family member or friend, sharing with them a specific appreciation memory that includes them, and telling them something you appreciate about their character.

jumpstart
LESSON 3

Staying Relational

Therefore if you have any encouragement from being united with Christ, if any comfort from his love, if any common sharing in the Spirit, if any tenderness and compassion, then make my joy complete by being like-minded, having the same love, being one in spirit and of one mind.
Philippians 2:1-2 NIV

Philippians 2:1-2 paints a picture of believers who receive such encouragement, comfort, tenderness, and compassion from being united with Christ that they are like-minded, one in spirit and in mind, and having a kindred love for one another. Paul says that knowing his friends are living this way will make his joy complete. That is powerful! We also often find this kind of bond difficult to achieve.

In Journey Groups, you'll be introduced to a number of concepts where neuroscience and faith have intersected. One of these concepts is "relational circuits," which captures the fact that our relational brain is actually a pathway, and there are factors that can enhance or interrupt the flow of information and emotions through the circuit.[1]

In *Rare Leadership*, relational circuits are explained very simply this way:[2]

> "...imagine that we have an 'on/off' switch on the back of our necks. When the switch is in the 'on' position, we are able to engage relationally and get in sync with the emotions of the people around us. However, when the switch is off, our capacity to remain relational disappears... This switch controls the relational circuits (RCs) in our brain."[3]

---

1 | Dr. Karl Lehman originated the concept of relational circuits.

2 | *Rare Leadership*, Dr. Marcus Warner, Dr. Jim Wilder.

3 | Ibid., p. 128

Although relational circuits do go "on" and "off," it's good to know that the switch is more like a dimmer switch; our relational circuits can go from bright to dim to off. The more quickly we recognize that our relational circuits are dimming, the easier it will be to restore them.

When our relational circuits begin to dim, we are losing connection with the most relational, creative, and mature parts of our brain. We aren't effectively processing our life experiences when this happens but are in a reactive frame of mind. What does it look like for our relational circuits to be off?

Here are some sure signs that the relational brain is going offline:

1. I'm not interested in what others have to say.
2. I wish someone would be quiet or go away.
3. I don't want to talk to someone I usually enjoy.
4. It seems like the other person is the problem.
5. I want to get away or argue, or I freeze.
6. My cravings are strong—I want to eat, drink, shop, or whatever I use to comfort myself.
7. I don't feel appreciation for things I usually appreciate.

What are some signs that my relational circuits are on?

1. I'm interested and curious about what others think.
2. I can see my part in the problem.
3. I welcome relational interactions.
4. My thinking is flexible, and solutions seem to flow easily.
5. My willpower seems operational, and I can make choices that are good for me and others.
6. I feel appreciation easily.[4]

The parts of our brain that help us connect relationally to other people also connect us to God, so building our awareness of our relational state will increase our awareness of our connection with Him.

Shalom is a Hebrew word translated as "peace," and shalom is an excellent way to describe how relational mode feels to our body and mind. Shalom includes not only the lack of conflict or upset, but a sense of "rightness" or alignment—that we are connected with God and people, that His way of thinking is available to us, and that living a life that pleases Him is a possi-

---

4 | Both of these lists are based on Lesson 4, *Belonging* module of Connexus curriculum, available from Life Model Works.

bility. Note that shalom doesn't mean our circumstances are perfect or even that we know exactly how to proceed in those circumstances. In John 4, Jesus told the Samaritan woman at the well, "The water that I will give [you] will become in [you] a spring of water welling up to eternal life," and in John 15, He invites us to live as branches attached to a vine. These beautiful promises are descriptions of a life lived in shalom, connected to Him and receiving from Him. How fascinating and beautiful that 21st century neuroscience has discovered that, indeed, our brains work most effectively and peacefully when our relational connections are open and receptive.

As believers, we have experienced times when we knew that it was God's will for us to be relational, but we simply felt unwilling and/or unable to do so. In every area of our life, we were designed to operate with relational circuits ON. When our relational circuits (RCs) are on, we have access to the parts of our brain that hold the will, that are creative and flexible in problem solving, that are able to sense how others are feeling, and that connect well with God and people.

Once we recognize that our relational circuits are dimming or off, we can take steps to restore ourselves to a more relational state. Because our bodies and our brains are constantly in communication, calming our body is helpful in bringing our minds back to peace and connection. How do we calm our body? Here are some helpful exercises:

1. Breathe deeply and slowly for a count of five. This brings oxygen to your brain and slows your heart rate. (Rapid, shallow breathing is a sign that your relational circuits are dimming or off.)

2. Close your eyes and notice if you have any tightness or tension in your body. Shrug your shoulders several times, swing your arms freely, bend forward from your waist; do any other stretches that will help you release muscle tension.

3. Sit with your eyes closed and let your hands rest in your lap, palms facing upward. Pray something like this: "Father, I release my worries and tension to You, and I receive what You have for me." If you have specific concerns or worries, you may want to intentionally release these to Him, and let Him know you receive whatever He has for you in exchange for your concerns.

Appreciation is an excellent indicator for the state of our relational circuits. When we are in relational mode, we can identify many things we appreciate, and we are generally comfortable expressing appreciation. In non-relational mode (RCs off), we may struggle to feel appreciation, even for people or situations we usually appreciate. This is because, when our relational circuits are off, we not only lose our sense of appreciation and relational connection, but we also lose our connection to relational and appreciation memories. Have you ever thought, "They always do this. This relationship is *always* hard"? This is an indicator that the connection to your relational and appreciation memories is dimming or gone. We restore this connection with the body exercises above and by "priming the appreciation pump" with our list of appreciation memories. What might this look like?

> Janet and her teenage daughter Margaret had a disagreement over what outfit Margaret could wear to a family event. As the discussion heated up, Janet realized she had fallen out of relational mode; her relational circuits were off. She told Margaret, "Let's take a few minutes to calm down and then talk about this some more."

> As she took some deep breaths and stretched to release the tension she noticed in her shoulders, Janet asked herself what she appreciated about Margaret. Not surprisingly, nothing came to mind, so she went to her bedroom and pulled out her Appreciation Notebook.

> She read through some entries about the beautiful sunset she'd seen earlier that week, something funny a neighbor's child did, and a Bible verse that particularly spoke to her. Feeling her tension begin to leave her body, Janet thought of how Margaret helped her with dinner some nights, and how they'd laughed at the antics of their puppy one morning.

> Janet closed her Appreciation Notebook, thanked God for Margaret, and went back to finish the discussion. With her relational brain back online, Janet was able to find a compromise with Margaret about her clothing, and their relationship was back on track.

As you go through your week, take notice of what circumstances affect your relational circuits both positively and negatively. You may want to set a reminder on your phone to check your RCs every few hours throughout the day; this helps you track how your sleep cycles, diet, exercise, time with God, and relational interactions affect your RCs, and how your relational state affects your overall quality of life. Noticing is the beginning of transformation!

PONDER, JOURNAL, AND DISCUSS:

1. Which signs of dimming relational circuits (#1-7, page 20) do you notice most often in yourself? Take some time to journal with God about this—what does He want you to know?

2. At least three times this week, try to practice the exercises on page 21 when you notice your relational circuits dimming. Which exercises seem to be most effective in restoring you to relational mode?

3. Read through the following verses. Ask God what He wants you to know about this portion of Scripture, and notice the thoughts that give you peace.

Psalm 16:5-11 ESV

⁵ The LORD is my chosen portion and my cup; you hold my lot.

⁶ The lines have fallen for me in pleasant places; indeed, I have a beautiful inheritance.

⁷ I bless the LORD who gives me counsel; in the night also my heart instructs me.

⁸ I have set the LORD always before me; because he is at my right hand, I shall not be shaken.

⁹ Therefore my heart is glad, and my whole being rejoices; my flesh also dwells secure.

¹⁰ For you will not abandon my soul to Sheol, or let your holy one see corruption.

¹¹ You make known to me the path of life; in your presence there is fullness of joy; at your right hand are pleasures forevermore.

jumpstart
LESSON 4

Listening to Jesus

Toward the end of each Journey Group, we take some time to quiet ourselves and "listen to Jesus." This simply means that we take some deep breaths, sit quietly, and notice what thoughts flow through our minds. Sometimes you will spend this time practicing being silent before God, sometimes you'll meditate on appreciation memories, and sometimes you will sense what might be God's voice. This is not intended to be a pressured time, but a time of practicing what it is like to interact with Him.

The book *Joyful Journey* describes hearing from God as "thought rhyming" and explains a mutual-mind state with God:

> "...Poetry in scripture does not rhyme sounds; it follows the Hebrew pattern and rhymes thoughts. This means that as God's poetry, our thoughts can rhyme with our Heavenly Father's. That is amazing! How can it work? We know that as we become intimate with someone, we begin to finish each other's sentences and thoughts. In a deep, authentic, mutual-mind state, we actually don't know where our thoughts stop and the other person's thoughts begin. This is exactly what can happen between God and us too. A mutual-mind state with God results in an emulation of His character and heart; we are showing the world the poet behind the poetry. As our mutual-mind state becomes stronger, we are able to live out our purpose of being created for good works."[1]

There are ways to facilitate achieving a mutual-mind state or thought- rhyming with God. The helpful booklet *Share Immanuel*[2] describes two "seats" where our awareness of God with us is enhanced, and one seat where awareness of God is very difficult. At the end of this lesson, you'll find the Immanuel Healing Diagram, a simple drawing which illustrates the seats we find ourselves in as we seek to connect with God.

---

1 | *Joyful Journey*, pp. 2-3, by Wilder, Kang, & Loppnow.

2 | *Share Immanuel*, by Wilder and Coursey. Available from THRIVEtoday or Life Model Works.

Let's consider this illustration. Imagine you are facing a tall hill, with God's presence shining like the sun above the hill. You notice three chairs sitting on the hill. At the bottom of the hill, there is a hard chair wrapped in thorns—the Pain Memories Seat. Would you be likely to sense God's presence while seated in this thorn-wrapped chair? No, you would be terribly distracted by the pain of the thorns pricking your legs. In the same way, when we sit in the midst of our pain and try to connect with God, our pain demands our attention, and we are unlikely to be aware of God's heart of love toward us. We are focused on getting relief for our pain.

As you move halfway up the hill, you notice a chair that looks fairly comfortable, although it is facing away from the sun of God's presence. When you appreciate the times when you felt joyful, peaceful, connected, or accepted, you are seated in the Appreciation Memories Seat. In this chair you are likely to feel God's presence "shining" on you, although you might not be aware it is Him. In this place of appreciation, you can ask Him, "What do You want me to know?" As you notice the thoughts that come into your mind, you may find that some of your thoughts feel peaceful and wise. This is thought-rhyming; you are thinking along with God.

The chair at the top of the hill is the Interactive Memories Seat; this is the home of the memories where we have sensed God's presence before and where we meet Him in the present. When we connect with Him through an Appreciation Memory, we have moved up the hill to the Interactive Memories Seat. As you think about the times when you felt connected to God, you may have a sense of His love, words or images may come to your mind, or you may simply feel joyful or peaceful.

Once you are in the Interactive Memories Seat, a place of peace and connection with God, you can ask Him about the painful events of life. From this place, you are more likely to maintain your mutual-mind state with Him as you engage with difficult or traumatic memories. You will learn more about strengthening your connection with God and receiving His healing in future lessons.

In our Journey Groups, we read what we sense from God to each other. There are many excellent reasons for this practice; here are a few:

- Reading our journaling out loud allows our brains to process the material in a different way, both logically and emotionally.

- Just as our mutual-mind with a friend can be flawed by misunderstandings, so can our thought-rhyming with God. It is helpful to share our journaling to see if they notice any content that differs significantly from the character of God. If you hear harsh, judgmental words from Him, your group members may remind you that our Father is loving and forgiving.

- Sharing our journal entries builds our understanding of each other and gives us a glimpse of the many ways God may reveal Himself to others. Our fellowship with each other deepens as we share.

PONDER, JOURNAL, AND DISCUSS:

1. What part of this lesson feels especially meaningful or important to you? Is there an aspect which seems challenging? Journal to God about this:

   a) "God, here's what feels important to me in this lesson, and why it seems important. Do You have anything to say about that?"

   b) "God, here's the challenging part, and here are a few words about that. How do You want to be with me in this challenge?"

2. Has your experience of "hearing God's voice" been similar or different from this lesson? What benefits do you anticipate from using the Three Seats method to assist you in connecting with God?

IMMANUEL HEALING
"God with Us"

Immanuel is based on the reality that God is always present with us and always has been.
Deut 31:8, Matt 28:20, Heb 13:5

Most of our memories are incomplete because we lack the awareness of God's presence. Our interpretations of life are distorted, bring pain and rob our peace.

GOD'S GIFTS & HELP IN THE PAST
The "Ah" Moments: A beautiful scene
... Kindness ... A Baby's smile ...
Warm cozy times ...

God is reaching out to interact with us.

words

pictures

thoughts

desires
body
sensations

emotional
shifts

"I remember ....
What do I need
to notice?"

"God ....
What do I need to
know about that?"

I can look toward God & sense His responses toward me. I feel that warm sense of God's personal interest in me.

THORN-FILLED PAIN MEMORIES SEAT

"No one is there for me, there's no sign of God, no peace"

The accumulation of life's experiences, traumas, & memories in which we are not aware of God's presence makes it increasingly difficult to be aware of God.

APPRECIATION MEMORIES SEAT

I cannot see God or be directly aware if the responses come from God, but I can see & appreciate the signs that God cares about me & my world.

INTERACTIVE MEMORIES SEAT

GOD'S HILL OF AWARENESS

There are three chairs you can sit in when relating to God. The best chair is at the top of the hill where you can see God more easily, but the appreciation chair is also good. Don't sit at the bottom of the hill in your pain!

Start your exploration & confusing times by returning to the memories when you know God the best and share a state of mind with God.

Your complete memories become a source of wisdom and reassurance of God's presence in your life & are like open windows for seeing God's active presence again in the present.

From **SHARE IMMANUEL** by James Wilder & Chris Coursey
2010 through Shepherd's House   www.lifemodel.org

heart-to-heart community
UNIT TWO

LESSON 1

We Create Belonging

And let us consider how we may spur one another on toward love and good deeds, not giving up meeting together, as some are in the habit of doing, but encouraging one another—and all the more as you see the Day approaching.
Hebrews 10:24-25 NIV

Better open rebuke than hidden love. Wounds from a friend are received as well-meant, but an enemy's kisses are insincere [...] Just as iron sharpens iron, a person sharpens the character of his friend.
Proverbs 27:5-6, 17 CJB

God created us for connection and relationship—from the very beginning. In creation Adam recognized that connection and relationship with Eve was what was missing for him. And, of course, God chose to enter into the human story through relationship.

It is interesting that when neuroscientists began to study the brain, they discovered that the brain works best when it is securely connected with others in a state of joy, which the brain defines as "someone's glad to be with me."

Secure connection creates an optimal state of joy and peace in our brains which builds our capacity to handle the stresses of life.

Another amazing discovery is that we are designed to create connection for those around us—not just to search for others to create it for us, but for us to create it for others. From conception, we are wired to create a place for us to belong. Did you know that the fetus actually creates the placenta as it attaches to mom? The baby creates a place for itself first, and then the mom's body responds.[1] This is a very intricate and special picture of the fact that God creates us with an ability to create belonging. God designed the family to develop this incredible ability and to identify and call out our special manifestation of this gift.

---

1 | www.nichd.nih.gov/research/supported/HPP/research_funding/human-placenta

Belonging is the joy we create around us, and because God is infinitely creative, there are infinite flavors of belonging...

- some of us create belonging by our warm smiles and hugs...
- some by the food we share...
- some by being aware of the physical needs of those who join us...
- some by creating beautiful art to enjoy visually...
- others by their incredible gift of music

Belonging could be called hospitality, but in our culture, we have a very limited definition of hospitality. Belonging is the invitation we extend to others to join with us, to share the good gifts God has given us, especially that of relationship.

Some are especially gifted at creating belonging for children, or the elderly, or the disabled. All of us want to welcome new people, but some have a special knack for that. Others may have a way of reminding old friends that they are still a delight. The beautiful thing about our individual style of creating belonging is that when we live in community, we create belonging for everyone—each person's style will resonate with certain others, and all feel an increase in joy and peace. We have a sense of God's shalom—that things are as they should be, even if life is not perfect.

Belonging is whatever we do that says to others, "Come join me! I'm glad you are here!"

At the fall, the first thing to suffer was belonging: "That woman *you* gave to me!" Suddenly the fact that Eve was so much a part of Adam brought shame and anger to him.

The refusal to create belonging brought about the first murder—Cain was so angry at his brother, and perhaps had such a sense of rejection, that he killed Abel, telling God, "Am I my brother's keeper?"

Can you think of other Bible stories in which there was a failure of belonging? What would it look like if belonging had been present?

- Abraham and Sarah rejected Ishmael and Hagar once Isaac was born. (Genesis 21).
- Jacob took advantage of his brother Esau's hunger. (Genesis 25)
- David arranged the murder of Uriah after David's sin with Bathsheba. (2 Samuel 11)
- Jonah refused to preach to the Ninevites. (Jonah 1)
- Peter quit eating with the Gentiles when other Jews came along. (Galatians 2)
- The Pharisees demanded Jesus' crucifixion. (Mark 15)

But God is a God of belonging, and we carry His image, so we see many examples of belonging in His Word as well.

- Abraham pleads with God on behalf of Sodom and Gomorrah (Genesis 18).

- Hagar hears God's voice and calls Him "'You are a God of seeing,' for she said, 'Truly here I have seen him who looks after me.'" (Genesis 16:13 ESV)

- Esau welcomes Jacob and his family when Jacob returns home (Genesis 33).

- Joseph provides for his family in Egypt (Genesis 45).

- The widow of Zarephath provides food for Elijah (1 Kings 17).

- Hosea is faithful and loving to his unfaithful wife (Hosea 3).

- God tells Israel to create a place for the foreigner who wants to worship Him (Isaiah 56).

- John the Baptist prepares the way for Jesus (Matthew 3).

- JESUS—His mission was to create a way of belonging for all people of every nation!
  - Created belonging for the outcasts, sinner, unclean, rejected. (Matthew 8:1-3, 28-34, Mark 14:3-9, Luke 9:10-17, Luke 10:25-37, Luke 19, John 9)
  - Offered belonging to Pharisees when He continually corrected their thinking. (John 9, John 10:22-39)
  - On the cross—created belonging for the thief and for John and His mother. (Luke 23:39-43, John 19:25-27)

- He gave us each a shared mission to create belonging for others—to tell the story of Immanuel—the God Who Is With Us—the God who creates belonging for each of us. (Matthew 28:19-20, Romans 15:14-16, 1 Peter 2:9-10)

When we are in pain, our ability to create belonging is affected, and we begin to look to others to make *us* feel welcome. Our world is full of people like this—and God intended the church to be the place that can restore people to their true identity—we are to be a life preserver that holds people upright until they regain their identity, until they reconnect with the lifeline—the true Vine.

Graham Cooke says that the church is the only institution that is created for the benefit of nonmembers. We are here not only to establish our own connection with God and people, to learn how to create belonging, but also to restore this ability to the world. One of the most important things about doing the work of helping to restore belonging is like being on an airplane—those equipped to help must put on their oxygen mask first.

How do we put on our oxygen mask?

Appreciation connects us with God, with the self that He created us to be, and it helps us create belonging around us. We truly enter His gates with thanksgiving. Appreciation is our oxygen mask!

Shalom is a state of peace where things feel like they are in the right balance—and appreciation is a sign that you are in shalom.

Growing our capacity for shalom and appreciation and learning to notice when we are feeling shalom and appreciation are important goals as we learn to practice creating belonging.

Appreciation is contagious—and it is spread through *stories*.

- The more we think about the people and moments we appreciate, the more appreciation we experience.

- When we share our appreciation stories, our appreciation multiplies.

- Appreciation stories are always stories about God, because whenever we experience appreciation, we are enjoying one of God's gifts.

- The more we focus our attention on appreciation, the more we tend to find and notice things we appreciate.

- As our focus changes, we have a new expectancy for good things in our life, and when they come, we notice them!

  > Finally, brothers, whatever is true, whatever is honorable, whatever is just, whatever is pure, whatever is lovely, whatever is commendable, if there is any excellence, if there is anything worthy of praise, think about these things. What you have learned and received and heard and seen in me—practice these things, and the God of peace will be with you. — Philippians 4:8-9 ESV

How did the Philippians pass on what they learned and received and heard and saw in Paul? *They told stories!*

As you practice telling Appreciation Stories in your daily life, you will create belonging!

How to tell your story:

- Keep it concise—don't need all the details.
- Briefly describe the situation.

- Use body language, eye contact, and voice tone to convey the emotions.
- Use emotion words.
- Tell how your body felt.

Begin to notice and practice creating belonging wherever you go!

PONDER, JOURNAL, AND DISCUSS:

1. What are some ways you create belonging in your daily life? Even if you aren't a very social person, God has given you some gifts of belonging. If you have a hard time identifying your style of creating belonging, ask God to reveal them to you.

2. What are some creative, practical ways you could implement more belonging in your life?

3. Have you started a list of Appreciation Memories? If not, start a list this week using an index card, a document on the computer, a note on your phone, or a small notebook.

LESSON 2

Quieting

For thus said the Lord GOD, the Holy One of Israel,
"In returning and rest you shall be saved;
in quietness and in trust shall be your strength."
But you were unwilling... Isaiah 30:15 ESV

But I have calmed and quieted my soul,
like a weaned child with its mother;
like a weaned child is my soul within me. Psalm 131:2 ESV

The LORD your God is in your midst, a mighty one who will
save; he will rejoice over you with gladness; he will quiet
you by his love; he will exult over you with loud singing.
Zephaniah 3:17 ESV

Quieting is the ability to settle ourselves down and calm our nervous system. It is a relational experience. We learn to soothe ourselves and quiet our souls by being soothed and quieted by others. Ideally, this will happen in infancy, as Psalm 131 expresses above—our mother comforts and soothes us when we are upset or overwhelmed, and in time, we learn to comfort ourselves. If our mother or another caregiver didn't pass on this essential skill, we can be thankful that our brains remain malleable throughout life. This means that we can gain this skill by being with those who offer to quiet with us—we learn from those who sit with us when we are upset without trying to fix our problems or from those we see quieting themselves in a difficult situation.

The 19 relational brain skills include three different types of quieting: Skill 2 is Simple Quiet or Soothe Myself. Skill 9 is Take a Breather, and Skill 15 is Quiet Interactively.

"Skill 2 [Simple Quiet] can be difficult to identify because replacement patterns are [often] socially acceptable. We replace quiet and rest with BEEPS [Behaviors, Events, Experiences, People, and Substances] in the form of busyness, work, sex, music, internet, television, and sugar. When this happens our world busily consists of the things we do, the items we buy, the people we know, the cars we drive, the places we work, [the churches we attend, ministry we do] or the brand of clothes we wear."[1] [Materials in brackets added.]

The lack of quieting skills is so common in our culture that many people feel agitated or nervous when they are quiet, which leads them to maintain a constant stream of busy work for their hands or mind. Practicing Simple Quiet exercises regularly can relieve this agitation so we can welcome moments of rest from our hectic schedules and begin sharing our new skills with others.

Most of us recognize that we need to quiet ourselves during negative emotions and during difficult circumstances, but our brains also need quiet after joyful interactions. Picture a child swinging on a swing set, constantly in motion, always on the way up or down, swinging gently past the resting point—regulating our emotional states is much like this. Joy is a high point as the child swings, and swinging back through the resting point leads to more high joy. We can picture high energy negative emotions like anger and fear as those moments when the swing goes too high and then jerks back into place; we quickly want to restore ourselves to a gentle swing from joy through quiet to more joy. And the low energy negative emotions like shame, sadness, disgust and despair? Those are the moments when the swing is stopped, and it takes some work to restore our back-and-forth rhythm.

We can take our swing analogy even further when we think of how we learned to swing; first someone pushed us, then they demonstrated for us, and with much practice, we gradually learned the coordinated back-and-forth leg motions that moved us into a satisfying rhythm. Perhaps you also learned how to swing with a friend, both of you standing together on the swing; this required the skills of synchronizing the motions of the swing with another person. This makes me smile both as I remember my childhood and as I think of how this relates to the complications of relationships, attuning with our people while we move through the challenges of life.

In our groups and communities, the skill of quieting is key to maintaining relationships and preventing ruptures. When our more mature group members demonstrate the skill of quieting for us, we learn to soothe ourselves before our emotions get out of control, and to practice Skill 9, Take a Breather. While Skill 2 is Simple Quiet—recognizing when our own emotions need to be quieted and also when we need some rest—Skill 9 is like double-swinging. In an interpersonal interaction, we recognize that either we or the other person needs to quiet. As Chris Coursey likes to say to his young sons, "The first

---

1 | *Transforming Fellowship*, Chris Coursey, p. 59

to stop wins!" We can be the first to stop when we recognize that a breather is needed and initiate a break in the action by simple words like, "Could we take a moment to breathe?" As you begin the practice of inserting breathers into high energy interactions, you'll find that you can remain relational for longer periods of time, even in the most intense discussions.

Skill 15, Quiet Interactively, means that we recognize when a joyful interaction has reached its peak and we lower the intensity. Tickling or wrestling are wonderful activities to allow children to burn energy, but they're also activities that illustrate the need to Quiet Interactively. As a child, my older brothers loved to tickle me until I was screaming or crying. Skill 15 was in short supply, and I suffered the consequences! It was encouraging for me to see my eldest brother tickle his children as long as they were enjoying it, then take a break until they ran to him for more tickles and giggles. I taught my children the motto, "It's only fun as long as everyone is having fun" so they would learn to recognize when joy spills over into anger or pain. Skill 15 is used to build trust; we are protectors when we use interactive quieting.[2]

As adults, Skill 15 provides a welcome break when groups are engaging in loud or energetic activities. We can watch for signs that the group's joy is reaching a peak, or we can make plans to alternate high energy, joyful activities with quieter ones. In family gatherings, this gentle, protective guidance can create an atmosphere that increases joy, models quiet, and builds strong bonds.

What are some ways that we can learn and pass on the three Quieting Skills?

- Introduce "Quiet Moments" at the dinner table, when taking a walk, or at other appropriate times. We can simply say, "Let's take a minute of quiet and see what we notice," "Can we sit quietly now that we've shared how our day went?" or "Let's be quiet a moment and see if we can sense what Jesus is doing right now."

- Have a code word or hand signal in your family or friend group to indicate when you feel the need for a micro-rest or longer break. For instance, giving the peace sign can let your friends know the energy level or emotional intensity is reaching an uncomfortable or peak level, and everyone can take a few deep breaths to "reset" the energy level of the conversation or activity.

- Set a timer for 30 minutes on your phone when you are at work or in other focused situations. When the timer goes off, breathe deeply, connect with Jesus, check your relational circuits, stand and stretch, walk outside or down the hall—do whatever is appropriate to quiet any tension you notice in your body, mind, or emotions.

---

2 | *Joy Starts Here*, p. 17, teaches about the concept of being a protector.

I love this story and quote from *Transforming Fellowship*:

> "Rest restores our relational capacity to persevere... When Elijah the prophet ran from Jezebel, fell down under the broom tree and prayed for death, he was at the end of his emotional rope. God sent an angel to feed Elijah two times, and the angel says, "'Get up and eat, for the journey is too much for you' (1 Kings 19:7b, NIV). Eventually God meets with Elijah and shows the prophet he is not alone. *Rest is the reminder that the journey is too much for us and we have limitations that require us to pause from interacting. Rest means, 'I need a breather.'* Fellowship should always lead to refreshing pauses and moments to rest while we stay in relationship."[3]

PONDER, JOURNAL, AND DISCUSS:

1. Read again this quote from Chris Coursey, *"...rest is the reminder that the journey is too much for us and we have limitations that require us to pause from interacting. Rest means, 'I need a breather.'"* (from 1 Kings 19:7) Did you learn any patterns of rest in your family of origin? Do you have opportunity for rest in your current living situation? What are some ways that you can make places for rest in your schedule?

2. Of the 19 relational brain skills identified by Dr. Wilder and the Courseys, rest or quiet (Skill 2) is best when alternated with joy (Skill 1). We need quiet and rest even from joyful interactions. This brings to mind the word "selah" in the Psalms. One interpretation of this word is to pause and notice what went before and what is coming.[4] Read through the verses at the beginning of this lesson and "selah" between them. Journal the thoughts that come to your mind.

---

3 | *Transforming Fellowship*, Chris Coursey, p. 61.

4 | Bullinger, E.W., *The Companion Bible*, Appendix 66.

Relational Styles, Part 1

As we've examined the heart-focused community skills of creating belonging, being protectors, and quieting, you may have noticed that some, many, or all of these skills sound foreign to you or are missing in your community and personal life. If so, you are not unusual. Relational skills are dropping out of modern society at an alarming rate, and this is often seen in the lack of connection in our communities. One of the underlying factors for disconnection and malfunctions in community is the *insecure relational styles* of community members. We will take the next two lessons to look at secure and insecure relational (or attachment) styles.

The concept of attachment or relational styles grew out of the research of John Bowlby (1950s) and later Mary Ainsworth (1970s), in which it was discovered that we each form a fairly consistent stance in approaching life and relationships based on our early connections with parents or other caregivers. Another way to say this is that our brains are wired with a certain way of connecting with others in our very early years of life. This attachment style or relational stance will generally remain in place throughout life unless we experience a sustained relationship that rewires the attachment center. Journey Group training is designed to help you pursue this rewiring process.

The four attachment styles identified by the research are known as Secure, Avoidant/Dismissive, Ambivalent/Distracted, and Disorganized. In the book *Relational Skills in the Bible*, Chris Coursey and Amy Brown describe these four attachment styles as follows:

> As Chris states in *Transforming Fellowship*, "Fears, hurts and emotional distance create insecure relational styles that will last for life unless we replace them." (p. 213)

Attachment or relational styles refer to the patterns of relating to other people that we develop early in life based on the way family members respond to our needs. Consistent warm responses instill resilience. When our needs are not met in a warm and timely manner, fear and pain are close behind. Let's look at the four attachment styles.

Secure attachment occurs when our parents respond consistently and affectionately to our needs. Mom and dad delight in us and help us feel seen, valued, calm, and confident. We learn that the world is a safe place where receiving and giving leads to joy and peace. People with secure attachment feel comfortable with their emotions and tend to have healthy boundaries.

When parents meet our needs in a timely manner but focus on our physical needs while minimizing emotional needs, we can develop a **dismissive (avoidant) attachment style.** This means that we are likely to dismiss our own emotions and needs as we grow older and do the same for the emotions and needs of other people. We become distant and will downplay the importance of relationships while staying emotionally disconnected from other people. Needs and emotions feel scary, unnecessary, and overwhelming.

On the other hand, when a parent interacts with his or her child based on the parent's needs and timing instead of the child's needs and timing, a distracted attachment develops. One way this can happen is when mom and dad consistently intrude and interrupt the child's play, then respond to the child's needs *on the parent's timetable* rather than the child's timetable. Parental inconsistency leads to a highly anxious reaction in the child where the child feels like he or she must be on high alert to notice and track the parent in order to determine if the child's needs will be met. This pattern is called a **distracted (ambivalent/anxious) attachment style** because we are distracted from life by our anxious desire to connect.

The last attachment style is known as a **disorganized attachment,** which occurs when our parents are the people we want to be close to, but they are also the people who frighten us. We desire close connection, but we fear what might happen if we get too close. This feels like a no-win situation for the child. We are just not designed for fear-based relationships![1]

In each attachment style, our "attachment light" responds to relational connection differently. The phrase "attachment light" refers to the nonverbal

---

1 | *Relational Skills in the Bible*, pp. 37-38.

expressions of our desire to attach, such as eye contact, smiles, and open body language. Our early childhood bonding experiences teach us how to regulate our attachment lights. In secure attachment, our attachment light goes on and off appropriately, depending on the depth of the relationship. With dismissive attachment, since emotional bonding wasn't strongly present, we learn to dim our attachment light, and may seem uninterested in connecting. On the other hand, with distracted attachment, our attachment light may seem to be on brightly all the time as we watch for opportunities to connect. This happens because our emotional needs were met on someone else's timetable rather than our own. Disorganized attachment will often lead to inappropriate function of the attachment light—we have learned to bond around fear, so we may actually light up for those that frighten us, but dim when others express a need for closeness.

As we review these styles, you may notice that you have characteristics from each attachment style; this occurs because most of us had several "attachment figures" in our early childhood years. It's possible to have a dominant attachment style but find that you react to certain people in a different way entirely. Let's look at some examples.

> Josie had a warm, loving mother who responded consistently to both her emotional and physical needs. With her mother, Josie always knew where she stood, and she learned to ask for what she needed without fear or shame. Josie had a *secure* attachment with her mother. On the other hand, Josie's father was a gentle, kind man, but he traveled extensively for his job. When he was at home, he was often busy catching up on paperwork and puttering in the garage or yard. Josie rarely interacted about emotional needs with her father, and when she did, he referred her to her mother. He was a nice man, but he seemed distant and not too interested in anything but her physical needs. Josie had a dismissive attachment to her father. As an adult, Josie has lots of close female friends, but finds it difficult to discuss emotional issues with her husband.

> Frank's father was warm and loving when he was taking his meds for bipolar disorder. When he went off his medications, he had an explosive temper. Frank loved his father but was very afraid of him as well. This led to a *disorganized* connection with him. Frank's mother was emotionally shut down and ignored her husband's violent outbursts for the most part. Frank's attachment to his mother was *dismissive*. As an adult, Frank avoids any form of confrontation with people in authority and is generally an easygoing man, if somewhat of a workaholic. When his wife or children pressure him for

emotional connection, Frank feels extremely anxious and occasionally blows up at them.

The study of attachment styles can last a lifetime and provide insight into many relationship struggles. This lesson is simply an introduction, so it is understandable if you are unsure where you fit. Things will become clearer as you learn more.

PONDER, JOURNAL, AND DISCUSS:

1. Ask Jesus what He wants you to know about your own attachment style and how it might be impacting your relationships. After you do this, take some time to meditate on an appreciation memory about a joyful interaction you've had in the past. This will help you reset your brain to appreciation.

2. Review the following Attachment Styles Checklist checklist, marking the items that seem to match your history and current behavior. Most people will mark items in several, if not all, categories. Interact with God about items that make you curious or concerned. Be sure to keep in mind that healing your attachment style is possible! **This is not a diagnostic tool**, but simply a way to notice characteristics of various relational styles.

Attachment Styles Checklist

SECURE	DISMISSIVE/AVOIDANT
I have close relationships with a number of people.	I have close relationships with very few or no one.
My "attachment light" is on in appropriate situations.	My "attachment light" is rarely on.
My emotions are felt at appropriate levels for me and others.	My emotions are on the back burner, ignored, or denied. I've been accused of not caring enough.
I'm willing to share my emotional needs with others.	I'm uncomfortable telling others my emotional needs.
I'm comfortable telling someone that they have hurt me.	I generally tell people I am "fine," even if I am hurt.
I feel like I am worthy of having my needs met.	I feel like I can take care of my own needs.

I feel like others will want to take care of my needs if they know about my need.	I feel like others can't or won't take care of my needs; my needs don't matter.
My parents were usually there for me as a child.	My parents were too busy, tired, depressed, or otherwise occupied to be there for me.
I feel like my relationships have a comfortable level of emotional sharing.	People sometimes want more out of me than I am willing to give emotionally.
I don't like conflict, but I know relationships will have some conflict, and I can handle it.	I usually avoid conflict.
I am able to balance work and relationships.	"Don't expect much" is one of my life philosophies.
I can set limits and say "no" pretty easily.	I am now or have been a workaholic, or I have a hobby that takes me away from home a lot.
I can treat myself without feeling guilty and without overdoing the treat.	I've had an issue with addiction at one time in my life (relied on something other than relationships for comfort).
DISTRACTED/AMBIVALENT	**DISORGANIZED**
I'm always seeking close relationships.	I alternate between being close and distant; may be a victim or a controlling person.
My "attachment light" is always on; I'm always seeking contact.	My "attachment light" is on until someone needs me; then I retreat or get angry.
I'm frequently or always emotionally needy or in high emotions.	I'm frequently emotional or needy, but I have a hard time expressing what it is I feel or need.
Sometimes my caregivers were there for me as a child, but not always. I felt like I needed to get their attention.	Sometimes my caregivers were there for me, but sometimes they scared me.
Sometimes I miss work/ school due to relational issues.	My childhood had a lot of drama at home.
I feel like others could take care of my needs if they just wanted to.	I feel like others can't/won't help with my needs.

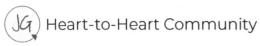

I've had a lot of relationship drama and/or failed relationships in my life.	I've had a lot of relationship drama and/or failed relationships in my life.
Sometimes people don't want to be as close to me as I want to be with them.	I have been involved in abusive relationships, either as abuser or abused.
I have low self esteem.	I have low self esteem.
I've had an issue with addiction at one time in my life (relied on something other than relationships for comfort).	I've had an issue with addiction at one time in my life (relied on something other than relationships for comfort).
I will put up with a LOT in a relationship rather than leave.	Sometimes I felt like I was a parent to my parent(s).
I am always the one trying to fix my relationships.	I find life overwhelming.
Other people find my needs overwhelming.	In certain relational situations I feel desperate to either get away or verbally attack the other person.
I have been the pursuer in a lot of relationships.	I don't like to fight, but find myself in a lot of angry relationships.

Relational Styles, Part 2

Here are some further descriptions of the Four Attachment (Relational) Styles:

- **Secure Attachment:** Because my early needs were met warmly and consistently, I view life as a generally safe place, relationships have a high value, I can repair ruptures in my relationships, and my decisions are more driven by joy, love, and connection than by fear. There is an appropriate balance in my reaching out for connection and in others reaching out to me.

Each of the following is considered an *Insecure* Attachment Style:

- **Dismissive/Avoidant Attachment:** As a baby and child, my physical needs were handled consistently, but not warmly, and my emotional needs may have been ignored or minimized. Other people sometimes accuse me of not caring; I care, but don't make a big deal out of relationships. I don't look to my relationships as resources, rather, I feel like I need to take care of myself. The high emotional needs of others make me uncomfortable, so I try to avoid emotionally intense situations. Generally, my friends reach out to me more than I reach out to them.

- **Distracted/Ambivalent Attachment:** My parents were more in tune with their own needs than mine, so I learned to watch carefully for potential relational connection. I tend to have strong emotional responses to life and some might see me as needy; I'm often the pursuer in relationships and feel hurt if others don't respond warmly. Relationships are a matter of urgent importance for me, and I feel like others have what I need emotionally.

- **Disorganized Attachment:** There was fear involved in my early bonds; either one of my parents was very fearful, or they were sometimes scary to me. I both desire and feel anxious about connection;

without intention, I've ended up in turbulent relationships at times. The world can seem a bit scary, confusing, and volatile; life is a big challenge.

All insecure attachment styles are fear-based rather than joy- and love-based. God created us for connection, and our early relationships actually wire our developing brain, so attachment styles that lead to disconnection or the fear of it affect not only our immediate relationships, but our entire approach to life. This is why it's important for us to set our hearts on pilgrimage to the place of secure attachment with God and people.

"Earned, secure attachment" occurs when we build secure attachments later in life, even though we didn't receive secure attachment in our early childhood. What does earned, secure attachment look like?

> An earned, secure attachment where our needs are met in a timely fashion instills joy, peace, resiliency and flexibility into our character and these qualities are expressed relationally. We navigate hardships with confidence. In times of distress we remember who we are and hold onto what is important. We are able to express our deepest-held values while keeping our relationships intact.[1]

I find it fascinating that a secure attachment looks very much like the character of Christ! We are created from the very relationship within the Godhead, "made in *Our* image." Is it any wonder that secure bonding with people and God enables us to live the life for which God created us? This life is loving, joyful, peaceful, tender with others, patient, able to suffer well, able to share truth in a kind way, and able to receive relational truths from others without losing our joy and peace. This is our goal, our pilgrimage, our journey.

What are some steps toward building a secure attachment to replace the insecure bonding patterns we may have received in childhood or because of painful relationships since then? The first step is to practice noticing the status of your relational circuits—secure attachment happens with relational circuits ON, so recognizing when our RCs are dimming and working to restore them quickly is Job One.

Jen Coursey tells us a bit about relational circuits here:

> Relational circuits are a specific part of our physical brain that, when functioning and working, help us feel connected with people. We have the *desire* to connect. When our relational circuits are dimmed or off, we lose our desire for connection and we no longer experience joy with the people around us. We no longer value or care about what others around us are

---

1 | *Transforming Fellowship: 19 Brain Skills that Build Joyful Community*, Chris Coursey, p. 215

thinking or feeling. We no longer correctly gauge our impact on others. Everything in life and relationships runs better when our relational circuits are on because we can be our best relational self to navigate the smooth or bumpy terrain of relationships. Thankfully, we all can learn how to recognize the moments our relational circuits are off then take the necessary steps to restore our RC's.[2]

We can restore our relational circuits by taking a break from stressful interactions, practicing the Shalom My Body exercises, relaxing our muscles, and looking for an appreciation memory. Being able to feel appreciation is a sure sign our relational circuits have been fully restored.

The second step of rebuilding your relational foundation is to Share Joy. Since relational joy means "I'm glad to be with you," we can share joy by expressing that "glad to be with you" feeling with those around us. We share our joy in mainly nonverbal ways—warm smiles, twinkling eyes, open body language, appropriate touch, as well as words that express that life is better together. Sharing joy begins to build our capacity to stay connected in challenging times. Picture a bucket, and imagine that each joyful encounter we have is filling our bucket little by little.

Another skill that fills our capacity bucket is Quiet. Our brains are designed to run in rhythms from joy to quiet, moving alternately through these states throughout the day. We can nurture this rhythm by noticing when our joy is at its peak, then taking a moment to quiet, which can be a simple deep breath and a silent break from the joy. Joy produces dopamine, which is a high-energy bonding chemical. Quiet releases serotonin, a low-energy neurotransmitter that produces a sense of peace. In our relationships, we bond to those with whom we share joy, and we learn to trust those who quiet with us.

We will gradually build secure bonds as we keep our relational circuits on and share moments of joy and quiet together. Our capacity bucket will be full on a more regular basis, and we'll feel ready for more advanced relational challenges.

My goal in life is to **learn to live as the person God created me to be in ever more difficult and complex circumstances**. Building secure bonds with God and a few people provides both the foundation and the enabling for this goal. I invite you to allow yourself time to focus on building this strong foundation so that everything you build upon it will be stable and secure.

PONDER, JOURNAL, AND DISCUSS:

Sometimes we read about God as our strength, shield, rock, or fortress, and we are imagining Him as "somewhere else." Read the following verses,

---

2 | Blog at www.thrivetoday.org by Jen Coursey, 5/3/17

considering your bond with God as a strength that you carry within you. Journal with God, asking Him what He wants you to know about these verses and His bond with you.

> **Psalm 46:1-3** NIV God is our refuge and strength, an ever-present help in trouble. Therefore we will not fear, though the earth give way and the mountains fall into the heart of the sea, though its waters roar and foam and the mountains quake with their surging.

> **Psalm 9:9** NIV The Lord is a refuge for the oppressed, a stronghold in times of trouble.

> **Isaiah 26:3-4** NIV Those of steadfast mind you keep in peace—in peace because they trust in you. Trust in the LORD forever, for in the LORD GOD you have an everlasting rock.

> **Isaiah 43:1b-3a** NRSV Do not fear, for I have redeemed you; I have called you by name, you are mine. When you pass through the waters, I will be with you; and through the rivers, they shall not overwhelm you; when you walk through fire you shall not be burned, and the flame shall not consume you. For I am the LORD you God, the Holy One of Israel, your Savior.

> **Philippians 4:6-7** NRSV Do not worry about anything, but in everything by prayer and supplication with thanksgiving let your requests be made known to God. And the peace of God, which surpasses all understanding, will guard your hearts and your minds in Christ Jesus.

LESSON 5

Listening to the Shepherd

BY NIK & KRISTY HARRANG

"My sheep listen to my voice; I know them, and they follow me" – John 10:27 NIV

"Learning to listen to God is a process that starts awkwardly and grows slowly but develops and matures until it is hard to see how you could ever have lived without it." – Rusty Rustenbach, *A Guide for Listening and Inner Healing Prayer: Meeting God in the Broken Places*

The above quote has proven true in our lives (Nik & Kristy Harrang). Several years ago, I (Nik) didn't think I could hear God really at all. Sometimes I would pray for someone and get a picture for them that would prove encouraging, but for me personally I had little to no confidence I could hear God. Now that has changed, and it has been one of the most revolutionizing things that has ever happened in my walk with God.

God Is a Communicative God.

Foundational to having two-way communication with the Lord is an understanding of His nature and character. In the beginning, God created the world with words. "The LORD merely spoke, and the heavens were created. He breathed the word, and all the stars were born."—Psalm 33:6 NLT (cf. Genesis 1:3ff). Then, when God sent His Son to save the world, He was referred to as the 'Logos' (Word) of God (John 1). God, by His very nature, is expressive, communicative, and verbal.

God is also relational—He created us for relationship with Himself. Healthy relationships are built on good two-way communication and the enjoyment of being together. It is one thing to know logically with my mind that God is with me, but when I seek Him and hear His voice, or feel Him wrapping His arms of comfort around me, that is when true peace and joy comes.

51

Giving God space to communicate to us that He is with us is life changing. As we give Him that space, He fills us with exactly what we need, whether it is comfort, guidance, wisdom, correction, empowerment, healing to our hearts, or simply the joy that comes from knowing He is present and glad to be with us.

We Are Designed to Hear God.

Jesus taught us that His sheep hear His Voice: "I am the good shepherd; I know my own and my own know me... My sheep hear my voice, and I know them, and they follow me"—John 10:14, 27. From this passage we see that He actually designed us with the capacity to be able to hear from Him! This is important for us to know because sometimes we can get stuck believing the lie that we can't hear Him. Consider the fact that humans are designed to be able to walk. Yet no one starts out walking—it takes time and practice to develop this ability. In a similar fashion, every one of God's children is designed to have a two-way relationship of hearing God and speaking with Him, but developing this usually involves time and practice.

God Promises to Speak When We Inquire.

> "This is what the LORD says, he who made the earth, the LORD¸who formed it and established it—the LORD is his name: ˙Call to me and I will answer you and tell you great and unsearchable things you do not know." Jeremiah 33:2-3 NIV

Throughout Scripture God tells us to talk to Him and expect Him to talk back! He wants us to seek Him for companionship, wisdom, and guidance. In the Old Testament, God was frequently provoked when Israel failed to seek Him. And yet, we also see Him respond with mercy and provision whenever they would humble themselves and turn to Him. We can be fully confident that as we come humbly to God, He will gladly receive us and respond (Hebrews 4:16).

Jesus taught that the Holy Spirit would guide and speak to us:

> "I have much more to say to you, more than you can now bear. But when he, the Spirit of truth, comes, he will guide you into all the truth. He will not speak on his own; he will speak only what he hears, and he will tell you what is yet to come. He will glorify me because it is from me that he will receive what he will make known to you." John 16:12-14 NIV

We Mature as We Grow in Godsight.

Contrast 'seeking God' vs 'thinking to yourself.' At times I forget to seek God and instead just do what makes most sense to me based on what I see and know. But turning to God acknowledges that He alone has wisdom, and that I value and depend on what He has to say more than what I think is best. In addition, as we seek God, we can better see His heart for the people and situations that we face. This development of Godsight (seeing from God's perspective) not only allows us to know God better and strengthens our relationship with Him, but it is also central to our process of maturing and growing to become more like Him.

HOW GOD SPEAKS TO US

There are many ways that God can communicate to us. He can share with us His majesty as we look at His creation (Psalm 19; Romans 1). God can instruct us through a verse in the Bible that jumps out at us (2 Timothy 3:16-17), and He can also use other people to speak to us (1 Corinthians 14:1-3, 26, 30). At the same time, God can also speak directly to us, especially when we invite Him to and take the time to listen. Here are some ways He might speak directly to our hearts:

- **Mental pictures** – Often these are faint, but not always.

- **A word or phrase** – You may 'hear' it internally or sense it.

- **An impression or a 'knowing'** – Sometimes you can simply 'see' something about a situation or person or get a sense of something.

- **A feeling or emotion** – Sometimes you might feel a strong emotion.

- **Heart vs Head** – Many testify to being able to discern God speaking more in their 'heart' than in their mind.

- **Scripture** – God may bring a Bible verse, biblical truth, or story to mind.

- **Interactive Journaling** – David in the Psalms, Habakkuk, and others asked the Lord questions and wrote down what they sensed in response.

Here's an example of how God spoke to me through an image. A few years ago, we had a woodpecker pecking at our house every day! I tried everything to get rid of it—I prayed against it, rebuked it in the name of Jesus, sprayed water at it, and searched Google for solutions. It was disrupting my sleep and my morning devotional times for two weeks. Finally, one morning I sat down and asked, "God, what do I need to be aware of about this woodpecker?" Immediately I saw a picture of a tarp hanging down from the roof in front of the area he pecked. I hadn't thought of this before and had no clue if it would work. But I dropped the tarp over the side of the roof and held it in place with a few bricks. We never heard from that woodpecker again! I had invested so much wasted energy in my methods, but it wasn't until I asked God that I received the wisdom I needed.

Another time I (Kristy) was praying with Nik over a wound in my heart. I was feeling discouraged and defeated. Nik asked God to show me what I needed to know, and immediately I had this picture in my mind of me as a little girl on the shoulders of my Heavenly Dad. We were outside something like a baseball stadium with a huge crowd surrounding us. God proudly paraded me through the crowd as I waved a white banner over my head. I began to cry as I experienced a strong "knowing" of how proud God was to call me His daughter and how deeply He enjoyed and loved me. That moment forever altered my understanding of how God felt about me!

There have been a number of times when we've prayed over a big decision we had to make. As we sought the Lord, He filled both of us with a deep peace and a sense of what we were called to do.

HOW TO POSITION YOURSELF TO HEAR GOD

- **Be still and know. (Psalm 46:10; Psalm 131:2)**

  Start with recognition that God is present and with you and desires to speak to you. Sit quietly in that amazing revelation.

- **Make sure your Relational Circuits are on.**

  Gratitude and praise are two of the best ways to do this (Psalm 100:4). Ask God for a positive memory to meditate on, journal about an attribute of God that blesses you, etc.

- **Ask Him to speak. (1 Samuel 3:10)**

  Present God with a specific question, or simply ask what He would like you to know right now.

- **Wait in silence and trust. (Psalm 62:1)**

  After you have prayed through the preceding steps, the thoughts that come to you are usually God's communication to you. You asked Him to speak. He said He would (Luke 11:9-13)! When you inquire of God, pay attention to the *first thing(s) that pop into your mind*. Don't edit or dismiss them. Even if images are faint or don't make sense, ask God to show you what He is saying. Even if words you hear sound like your own thoughts, trust that God is speaking.

- **Write down what impressions God gives you. (Habakkuk 2:2)**

  Steward what God gives you, and He will give you more. Often things that seem faint and only moderately impacting become clearer and resonate more deeply as we write them down and as we share them with others. Also, this allows you to record important aspects of your growing relationship with God.

God allows us to attune with Him, to tune in to His thoughts, and each of us does this in slightly different ways from each other. The more time we spend gently experimenting with these tools, the more we will begin to recognize the various ways He tends to speak to us. Intimacy is built by time spent together.

What Can Hinder Connection with God or Our *Awareness* of Him?

Notice that word *awareness*—there are far more things that will hinder our *awareness* of God's presence and His speaking to us than will actually affect our connection with Him. We are a vine, always connected to the branch, but we often lose awareness of that connection.

- **Family history**

  If we grew up in a family that didn't have an expectation of hearing God, we probably haven't expected to hear Him speaking to us personally. As with all family weaknesses, we can grow beyond our history.

- **Fixed expectations**

  When we box God in by predetermining what He will say or what kind of answer He will give us, we limit our capacity to hear Him. Being wide open to hear whatever He wants to say will best position us to hear His voice.

- **Over analyzing (Proverbs 3:5-6)**

  This was my biggest challenge in hearing God. I would try to assess everything I heard and determine with my mind if it could be God. In order to allow God's thoughts to flow through me, I had to learn to let go of my own mental processing for the moment.

- **An unsurrendered will (John 7:17)**

  If we are stuck in sin or unforgiveness, or are unwilling to yield fully to God, we will limit what we are willing to hear from Him. God is well able to speak to us when we are unsurrendered, but we are less able to recognize Him or accept Him. Choosing to surrender all to Him will better enable us to hear whatever He wants to say.

How Do You Know You Are Really Hearing God? (1 Thessalonians 5:20-21)

- **You won't, and it's okay.** We frequently have a variety of voices floating through our minds, including that of God. Set your mind at ease by recognizing that what we receive will most often be a mixture of our own thoughts, God's thoughts, and distractions from our life. This is why we need heart-focused community; we were never meant to hear Him in isolation from other healthy believers. Sheep recognize their shepherd's voice best when they are with their flock.

- **It will line up with the Bible.** (*Note: God will never contradict today what He has already spoken in His written Word.*) This is just one more reason why we should be in God's Word at some level, ideally every day. By being immersed in the Word of God you get to know God's heart, His ways, and how He works, so when God speaks into your life here and now, you know if it is in line with His nature and character.

- **It will bear witness with our spirit and produce shalom/peace. (Romans 8:16, Colossians 3:15)** You have the Holy Spirit in you, and if you are walking with Him, you'll often just 'know' what God is saying versus your own thoughts. Also, while God might sometimes ask us do things that are stretching and cause discomfort, the overall sense should be one of peace, hope, and encouragement.

- **Other solid Christians confirm it sounds like God. (2 Corinthians 13:1)** As we share God's revelation to us, mature Christians around us can 'bear witness' in their hearts that what we are hearing resonates with God's character and produces shalom/peace.

- **It is consistent with God and His character vs. with the works of the sinful nature or the enemy.** The voice of God will be in line with the fruit of His Spirit (Galatians 5:22-23, cf. James 3:17-18). If fear, shame, or other negative emotions come, or condemning or critical thoughts come, they are not from God (see Romans 8:1-2, 1 John 4:18).

PONDER, JOURNAL, AND DISCUSS:

1. Were there any new or surprising thoughts in this lesson? Ask Jesus what He wants you to know about these surprising thoughts.

2. In what ways have you heard from God? Ask Him to bring more examples to mind over the next week or two and write them down. You may have heard His voice more frequently than you realized.

3. Does this lesson mention ways to tune in to God that you haven't tried? Over the next few weeks, take time with Him and ask Him to communicate to you in ways that you haven't noticed or tried before. For instance, ask Him to awaken you to images or words

that occur to you, or sights you see as you go about your day. Begin to notice sensations and emotions, and ask Him about them. As you read the Word, stop whenever a word or phrase feels important, and notice what thoughts arise. Journal about these experiences, and share with a mature friend or family member.

I'm enlingnee up the boch
I methods
waday of this is one of
the [?] God will use.
to build the relationships
& invite the [?] need
that will be part of
a new body
[?] group the body of Christ

LESSON 6

A Community of Transformation for All[1]

In this unit, we have learned how creating belonging, quieting, connecting with Jesus, and relational styles affects the type of community we will show to the world. When these pieces are in place, we will be a community of transformation for *all* members.

In Isaiah 11, we see a description of the Kingdom rule of Jesus. Read slowly through this description of Jesus and His Kingdom:

> "There shall come forth a shoot from the stump of Jesse, and a branch from his roots shall bear fruit. *And the Spirit of the LORD shall rest upon him, the Spirit of wisdom and understanding, the Spirit of counsel and might, the Spirit of knowledge and the fear of the LORD...* The wolf shall dwell with the lamb, and the leopard shall lie down with the young goat, and the calf and the lion and the fattened calf together; and a little child shall lead them. The cow and the bear shall graze; their young shall lie down together; and the lion shall eat straw like the ox. The nursing child shall play over the hole of the cobra, and the weaned child shall put his hand on the adder's den. *They shall not hurt or destroy in all my holy mountain; for the earth shall be full of the knowledge of the LORD as the waters cover the sea.*"[2]

It's clear from this passage that the Kingdom of God is meant to be not only a place of protection for the weak, but also a place of transformation for both the prey and the predator. We see this truth in the book of Acts—who could be considered more of a predator than Saul, breathing threats and murder against the disciples? We've read this story so many times that we've

---

1 | Portions of this lesson are taken from Dr. Jim Wilder's lecture on "Why We Shouldn't Create a Safe Space," Transform Conference, April 2018.

2 | Isaiah 11:1-2, 6-9 ESV, emphasis added

lost the heart-stopping sense of suspense that must have gripped the disciples when they heard that Saul had become a believer—could this be true, or was it a clever ruse to infiltrate their ranks and drag them all off to Jerusalem in chains? Had the predator been transformed into a protector? God's plan was revealed; He would transform the wolf into a lamb and bring him into their midst as one who would give his life rather than betray them and their Savior.

Even if we discount Saul's transformation because of its supernatural genesis, we can see predatory behavior in the "circumcision party," those who expected all new believers to become Jews. In 1 Corinthians, we also see Paul addressing jealousy, strife, boasting, divisions, and favoritism in the church, and then reminding the people to forgive, comfort, and reaffirm their love for the one who has sinned. A thorough reading of Acts and the Epistles makes it clear that the early church was confident in God's ability to use *them* to bring transformation to the weak and the strong.

Have we lost faith that the Kingdom of God here on earth is a place of transformation for all?

In *Joy Starts Here*, the authors explain that we all notice the weaknesses in ourselves and others, but we have widely varying responses to those weaknesses. The three responses to weakness described in *Joy Starts Here* are Protector, Predator, and Possum.

> **Protector:** A protector is one who helps others to grow their Christlike identities and maintain those identities under pressure. Protectors notice weakness and look for ways to protect the weak. A gentle protector will confront predatory behavior and its harmful impact on a community and will protect the group from predators until they are transformed into protectors.

> **Predator:** Someone who monitors weaknesses looking for a way to gain a personal advantage is a predator. All of us have a predatory system inside our brains which will develop with little to no training. Without secure bonds and relational skills, our response to weakness will be predatory. In a protective community, our predatory ways begin to transform as we develop secure bonds and learn relational skills. Transformed predators become very strong protectors.

> **Possum:** A possum is someone who thinks like a predator ("Weaknesses will get you eaten"), does not want to be a predator, but lacks the skills to be a protector. Avoiding attack becomes a possum's central preoccupation, motivation, and even identity. A possum plays dead or tries to hide so as not to be eaten. In a protective community, possums begin to model themselves after the protectors, picking up relational skills

and growing secure bonds. Transformed possums become very compassionate protectors.

In *Joy Starts Here*, the authors identify the Transformation Zone as a place where there is multi-generational community, a tender response to weakness, and an awareness of God's presence. Transformation happens not in an environment where everything is ideal, but in an environment where everything can be *faced*, and is faced together. When we have the weak and strong together, facing their fears and weaknesses honestly and seeking God's perspective on everything, transformation is possible for all. The truly mature members of the group (protectors) guide all of us in building strong, secure bonds with God and each other. As our bonds strengthen, we learn protective ways of handling fear and weakness, rather than predator or possum methods.

This kind of protective community was exemplified in the New Testament in instances such as the time Paul opposed Peter in Antioch when Peter stopped eating with Gentiles after the conservative Jews arrived. Paul was calling out Peter's "possum" behavior, his fear of the conservative Jews, and addressing the predatory behavior of the Jews as well. Paul was reminding Peter of his identity as a protector of the Gentile believers and of their freedom from religious bondage. Can you take a moment to imagine the emotions of the Gentile Christians on this occasion? What were their feelings when Paul stood up for them in this way, when he refused to join in the religious and racial snobbery being practiced? Paul was standing firm for the Kingdom as a place where the lines between predator and prey were erased and the table was set for both leopard and lamb.

We will learn more about the role of protectors in Lesson 7.

PONDER, JOURNAL, AND DISCUSS:

1. Protector, Possum, Predator: Which one of these descriptions do you identify with the most? What about when you are in pain, such as anger or fear? How can the various things you've learned in Journey Groups help you move more toward Protector on the continuum? [Check In, Appreciation, Listening to Jesus, Freedom, Identity, Walking in the Spirit, etc.?]

2. The Transformation Zone is described as (1) multi-generational community, (2) tender response to weakness, and (3) awareness of God's presence. Another way of saying this is that transformation happens when we have the strong and weak together, facing fears together, and getting God's perspective on everything. Have you experienced a group that is like this? Which parts are most present in your current fellowship? Which are most missing? What are some first steps to bringing these components to your family or church?

LESSON 7

The Importance of Protectors in a Transformative Community

In every community, there will be a mix of protectors, predators, and possums. For that matter, in every person, there exists a mix of protector, predator, and possum thoughts, feelings, and behavior. As we grow into our true identity as the children of God, we will come to exhibit protector behaviors more consistently. This means that when we notice weakness in others, we will feel tender toward their weakness, but we'll also have the willingness to help our brother or sister arise out of their weakness and become the person God has created them to be. This is what it means to be a protector.

Most of us have a genuine desire to be a protector, but walking this out requires a fairly high joy capacity, the ability to keep relational circuits on and to quiet big emotions, emotional maturity, and skill in seeing people from God's perspective. We haven't yet discussed all of these tasks and skills, but it's good to begin noticing where you are on the spectrum of gaining protector skills and to begin moving your community or group toward being a place where weaknesses are a signal for growth rather than a place of shame or judgment.

Building Capacity

As individuals and as a community, growing our joy capacity should be considered a top priority. A high joy capacity enables us to remain our best selves in challenging, frustrating, difficult circumstances; it allows us to suffer well when needed; it enables us to do the hard things that are needed to build a healthy community of protectors.

How do we build joy capacity? Below are four key elements to practice individually and corporately:

- Notice and build your ability to keep *relational circuits on*.
- Practice *appreciation* throughout the day.
- Increase your capacity to *quiet* during difficult circumstances.
- Look for opportunities to build *joy* as often as possible.

As an appendix at the end of this book, you'll find an exercise called "Reset Your Brain's Normal to Joy, Appreciation, and Quiet," which is designed to help you reset your brain's normal to joy, peace, and appreciation. If your community practices this exercise regularly for 30 or 60 days, there will be a noticeable increase in joy capacity for individuals and for the group as a whole.

Who Are We?

Every community has a group identity[1] which can consist of things like common interests, characteristics, or behavioral expectations. It is a natural part of our development that we feel a strong desire to identify with a group; God created us this way. Another way to describe group identity is "what it is like me and my people to do" in any given situation. As believers, our group identity will include Christ-like traits that we desire to express, and our example and encouragement to one another are key elements in our growth toward life as the people God created us to be.

Hebrews 10:23-25 ESV reminds us of how important we are to each other:

> "Let us hold fast the confession of our hope without wavering, for he who promised is faithful. And let us consider how to stir up one another to love and good works, not neglecting to meet together, as is the habit of some, but encouraging one another, and all the more as you see the Day drawing near."

Reading this passage in the Passion Translation amplifies the beauty of staying strongly connected with our people:

> "So now we must cling tightly to the hope that lives within us, knowing that God always keeps his promises! Discover creative ways to encourage others and to motivate them toward acts of compassion, doing beautiful works as expressions of love. This is not the time to pull away and neglect meeting together, as some have formed the habit of doing, because we need each other! In fact, we should come together even more frequently, eager to encourage and urge each other onward as we anticipate that day dawning."

As we are growing in our ability to live as protectors of one another's weaknesses, it is wise to proactively discuss our group identity. Who are we? How do we want to respond to difficult circumstances? What fruit of the Spirit do we need to develop? What strengths do we have as a group? Where do we need to grow in our ability to express this group identity? How will we help each other grow?

Although we'd love to think that every group would naturally know what it means to be protectors, the fact that we've all grown up with a different "normal" in the way we've seen weaknesses addressed means that a set of general

---

1 | Group identity is discussed in *Rare Leadership* by Drs. Warner and Wilder.

guidelines may be needed. The adaptation of Journey Group guidelines at the end of the lesson may be helpful for your group.

Being Authentic and Transparent

As a group grows in its ability to protect one another, there is increased safety to be authentic and transparent about weaknesses. However, since we understand that all of us have some predator tendencies that may arise, it is wise to move slowly in sharing weakness. Those group members who have greater capacity may want to share first, allowing others to see an area where we need growth. For instance, one group member might let others know, "I'm recognizing that I have difficulty keeping my relational circuits on when my toddler has a temper tantrum." This gives the group an opportunity to practice gentle protection, listening carefully without offering advice, praying consistently for this member, observing confidentiality about this sharing of a weakness, and checking in regularly to see how things are going.

As group members begin to share their weaknesses and the group is able to respond as protectors, the level of transparency and authenticity can increase.

If a group member shares a weakness and we see predatory responses (chastising or condemnation, gossiping about the weakness, giving unsolicited advice, etc.), as protectors, we gently remind those with the predatory responses, "Our group is one that protects." We do this gently because *predatory behavior is a weakness.* This is one of the biggest challenges in building a protective community that is committed to bringing transformation—while we must protect each other from behaviors that look strong and predatory, we remember that the need to engage in predator or possum behavior is a weakness. This is where our guidelines serve us well, providing the words that help us remind one another that we are protectors.

Here are some Protector Guidelines.

PROTECTING ONE ANOTHER

1. We protect one another by observing confidentiality. What is shared between group members (whether in a group meeting or personally) is not discussed with anyone else without permission.

2. We protect one another by giving each member time to share as they are comfortable.

3. We protect one another by not overwhelming each other with intensity or by monopolizing the discussion. We allow others to let us know if we are overwhelming.

4. We protect one another by listening to understand each other rather than to correct or share our opinion. (James 1:19—"quick to hear, slow to speak")

5. We protect one another by giving advice only when it is requested.

PONDER, JOURNAL, AND DISCUSS:

1. Ask Jesus to bring an appreciation memory to your mind. Spend three minutes fully entering into that memory. Move to question 2.

2. Review Hebrews 10:23-25 from The Passion Translation, and ask Immanuel what He would like you to know about this description of community. Notice and write down the thoughts that arise.

3. Review the guidelines "Protecting One Another." Ask Jesus where He wants to work with you on your growth as a protector. Make note of the thoughts that might be from Him.

F.I.S.H.
welcome back to
relational discipleship
UNIT THREE

LESSON 1

Introduction to Relational Discipleship

Let's take a step back in time and place to Galilee in the 1st century. How would Jesus' followers have understood His statement to "go and make disciples of all nations"? The word "disciple" means a learner, particularly one who learns by study, observation, and imitation of the teacher's life. In the 1st century Jewish world, discipleship was defined by relationship. Mark 3:14 indicates that Jesus appointed the twelve disciples "that they might be with Him," and Luke 6:40 states that the disciple who is fully trained "will be like his teacher." In Acts 4:13, after Peter and John spoke boldly to the rulers, elders, scribes and high priests, it says that "they recognized that they had been with Jesus ."

In Dr. Marcus Warner's webinar, "Fixing the Broken Discipleship Factory," he examines the fact that the 21st century church isn't producing disciples whose lives make it obvious that they have "been with Jesus." Where did the church get off track and how can we restore relational discipleship?

In the first few centuries after Christ's death, Christianity passed from person to person, family to family, and town to town through relationship. Christians were persecuted for their faith and the church was largely a grassroots underground movement. Due to the relational nature of their faith and the effects of persecution, believers relied on each other for finances, housing, spiritual growth, and emotional support.

It's not surprising that this relational faith is consistent with what we now know about attachment and belonging—we are created by God to be strongly motivated to live and believe like those to whom we have strong connection. God designed us to be in relationship with Him and with those who love Him.

In the 4th century A.D., Roman emperor Constantine first allowed and then promoted Christianity in the empire, and within 50 years emperor Theodosius had made Christianity the state mandated religion. With this ruling, everyone born in the Roman Empire was considered a Christian, and the relational component began to fade.

As a state-mandated religion, Roman Christianity became an institution rather than a relational entity and began to spread by building more churches rather than relationships being formed around Jesus. Christendom as an institution largely replaced Christianity as relationship. Christendom was found to be an effective way to control citizens, as people were expected to conform to a code of beliefs and behavior set forth by the state.

In the Reformation of the 16th century, Protestants broke with the Roman Catholic church but replaced Catholic Christendom with Protestant state-mandated religions, and Christendom continued. If it were not for the invention of the printing press, this state of affairs might have continued for much longer than it did. The printing press brought the Bible to the laity as well as spreading new philosophical thoughts throughout Europe.

This spread of philosophical thought resulted in the Enlightenment—a time of questioning what is important, what is truth, and what defines us. René Descartes' famous phrase, "I think, therefore I am" infiltrated both ecclesiastical (church) and philosophical conversation, and truth moved to the center of the Christian faith. No longer was faith based on relationship (as in the early church) or on politics (as in Catholic and Protestant Christendom), but on the content of one's beliefs.

As a result of these changes, it was understood that Christian transformation came about from the combination of good Reason with good Choices.

REASON + CHOICES = TRANSFORMATION

Discipleship became a matter of providing the right information and guiding disciples to the right choices. Intelligence and willpower were more important than relationship, and those who had high intelligence and strong willpower were successful disciples. This formula worked well for the strong in the church but left the weak feeling shamed and left out. Even the strong suffered shame when they slipped and made poor choices. Rather than building intimacy in relationships, this formula created a culture of perfectionism, hiding, and judgment.

In *Rare Leadership*, Drs. Marcus Warner and Jim Wilder offer a new formula based on Scripture and neuroscience:

IDENTITY + BELONGING = TRANSFORMATION

"Who we are determines what we will do and identity [the part of the brain that controls identity] operates faster and more powerfully than [the part of the brain that controls] choices."[1]

In Journey Groups, we intentionally grow a place of belonging and identity so that transformation occurs naturally and relationally. We are helping one another grow in Freedom, Identity, Walking in the Spirit, and Heart to Heart Community. In this way, we create an ever-expanding community of relationship in which we grow in Christlikeness together. Because the Life Model[2] explains the components needed for full, healthy life and relationships, we will also examine these foundational concepts (a place to belong, the opportunity to give and receive life, healing from trauma, maturity, and knowing our heart and God's heart). Journey Groups provide a model of relational discipleship that you can easily incorporate into your daily life.

We will delve into the elements of discipleship in more detail in future lessons of this unit. For now, we will review these elements briefly:

> **Freedom:** We have died with Christ (buried with Him) so we can be set free from the world, the flesh and the devil. It was for freedom He set us free (Gal. 5:1), so we will learn how to throw off everything that hinders and the sin that so easily entangles (Heb. 12:1). Helping one another walk in freedom means we are gentle with one another's weaknesses and learn to keep relationships bigger than problems.
>
> **Identity:** Just as we died with Christ, we were also raised with Him (Col. 3:1). We have a new identity, but learning to walk in this new identity can be a challenge. Not only do we have a new individual identity (child of God), we also have a new group identity (the body of Christ, the family of God). As our sense of identity and belonging grows, we will be transformed.
>
> **Walking in the Spirit:** As children of God, our Father reveals His perspective on life to us and we no longer walk by our flesh (our own choices and reasoning), but by His Spirit (Gal. 5:16). His Word comes alive to us and His Spirit enables us to love one another sincerely (1 Pet. 1:22) and to walk in our identity as His children.
>
> **Heart to Heart Community:** Returning to relational discipleship as Jesus modeled means that we show God's love to each other practically, that we model walking in the Spirit,

---

1 | *Rare Leadership*, p. 46. (brackets added, italics removed)

2 | *Living from the Heart Jesus Gave You*, Dr. Jim Wilder and others

in freedom and in our identity in Christ, and we welcome both the weak and the strong into our fellowship. Our hearts are knit together in love, and God will use us to bring His transformation to the world.

PONDER, JOURNAL, AND DISCUSS:

1. What forms of discipleship have you experienced? What were the strengths and what did you gain from the experience? What seemed to be missing, if anything?

2. What do you hope to gain from this relational discipleship experience?

3. Were there any phrases or thoughts that felt new or particularly important to you in this lesson? What were they? Highlight them or write them in your journal.

LESSON 2

Gaining FREEDOM

Galatians 5:1 NIV says, "It is for freedom that Christ has set us free. Stand firm, then, and do not let yourselves be burdened again by a yoke of slavery."

I recently watched a documentary about a man who was released from prison after a wrongful conviction. Although this man was free, his experiences in prison and his lack of experience with the outside world had a tremendous impact on his ability to live as a free man. Many Christians live in a similar conundrum—free in Christ but hindered by their life experiences.

At the cross, Christ redeemed us into freedom from sin, Satan's schemes, and the entanglements of the world. These are now accomplished facts. However, Satan is the Father of lies, and he will do all he can to twist our life experiences and hinder our ability to live in freedom.

In *Understanding the Wounded Heart*, Marcus Warner lays out the progression of Satan's common strategy for hindering freedom in our lives:[1]

PROBLEM	SOURCE	OBSERVATION
Wounds	World	It is impossible to live in a fallen world without being wounded.
Lies	Devil	The impact of the past is not in the size of our wounds, but in the power of what they mean to us.
Vows	Flesh	A vow is an attempt by the flesh to take control of life and keep ourselves from further pain.
Strongholds	Wounds, Lies, Vows	Strongholds keep us from trusting God. They are barriers to God's love and force us to live in our own strength.

---

1 | Table from page 29 of *Understanding the Wounded Heart*, 2nd Edition

In this lesson, we will discuss solutions to help us walk in freedom—to overcome the effects of past wounds and to process future wounds so that we don't lose our freedom.

It is important to understand that *our brain experiences, stores, and processes the memories of our wounds in two very different ways and we need solutions for each of these ways.* Our brain stores the facts and narrative memories of our experiences on its slow track, while the emotions of "how it felt" and "was I alone" is stored in the fast track. The fast track is the "Control Center" for the brain.[2] In layman's terms, this means that our bonds and emotions drive our decisions more than the information we know. It is also good to understand that brain scans have revealed that the same part of our brain is active when we interact with God as when we interact with people. This means that the healing of our connections with people and God have a synergistic effect—what helps our interaction with people also helps our interaction with God!

This seemingly very "unspiritual" neuroscience information is key to understanding how to fully process wounds, lies, and vows so that strongholds are removed and our relationship with God can bloom and prosper.

<u>Wounds</u>: When we are wounded, the "facts" of what happened and the verbal story we tell are stored in the slow track of the brain. However, our fast track stores how the experience felt in our body and emotions, whether it is considered good, bad, or scary, and whether we felt alone in the experience.

Three common types of wounds are:

1. *"A" Trauma:* Absence of the good things we need like consistent love, laughter, physical affection, boundaries, food, shelter, clothing, and security.

2. *"B" Trauma:* Bad things that happen to us, like physical, emotional, or sexual abuse, war/refugee situation, divorce in the family, serious illness of self or family member, and abandonment.

3. *Comparison/ Perception:* Pain resulting from negative comparisons, whether by ourselves or important people in our life, and pain resulting from faulty perceptions of reality.

God is with us when the wound hits, ready to comfort us, strengthen us, and "work all things together for good"[3] in spite of the pain and negative consequences of the wound. Our ability to sense and trust His presence is affected by not only the truth we know, but also by the experiences we have had in the past.

---

2 | To learn more about the slow and fast tracks of the brain, read *Rare Leadership* by Drs. Marcus Warner and Jim Wilder.

3 | Romans 8:28

<u>Lies</u>: Satan stands by when we are wounded, ready to tell us lies about the meaning of the situation, the people involved, ourselves, the world, and God. We know that God is also near at hand, and our ability to receive God's comfort and love is affected by the previous lies we have believed, vows we have made, and strongholds which now exist. We will talk later in this lesson about "lie-proofing" our hearts and minds.

We may receive lies on the conscious, slow track from the words of those around us ("You will never amount to anything"), from teaching we have received ("God will punish your mistakes"), from the world ("If you aren't beautiful, athletic, or smart, you can't be happy"), and from our faulty understanding of God, His world, and His Word ("God must be angry at me; that's why I can't get a job."). On the fast track, lies arise from experiences and feelings from the past. For instance, if my mother is often anxious, I may have a pervasive fear that "the world is a very dangerous place." Satan can whisper lies to both the fast and slow track, whether it is through others, the world, or our own mind. We can receive freedom from lies in both tracks!

<u>Vows</u>: Lies which are not processed quickly often lead to vows of protection because we want to avoid future pain. God created our minds so that we can learn to relationally process the pain of our wounds, but when we don't have this skill, lies send down deep roots and create vows. We may consciously make vows on the slow track such as "I will never trust anyone again," or our fast track may have deeply ingrained feelings that act like vows, for instance, "My abuser was a jolly man, so I am intensely nervous or angry around jolly men." Vows feel as if they protect us from pain, but in reality they limit our ability to connect deeply with God, family, and friends.

<u>Strongholds</u>: "A stronghold is an area of bondage in which we are not free to live with joy and peace. It is characterized by compulsion, restlessness, hopelessness, addiction, and self-deception."[4] Because strongholds have formed over a period of time, they always involve both the fast and slow tracks of the brain. We have strong emotions like fear and anger (fast track) that drive us to make choices that violate our beliefs (slow track).

SOLUTIONS THAT BRING FREEDOM TO BOTH TRACKS:

There are solutions which bring relief to the slow track and others which help us on both tracks. It's interesting that other than interacting directly with God, most "fast track" solutions actually happen as a process over time. God sometimes brings clarity and truth to both tracks very quickly.

- **Listening prayer:** Interaction with God will be our bookends; when we are wounded, we start by telling God how we feel about this wound and asking Him what He wants us to know. Then we notice what

---

4 | *Understanding the Wounded Heart*, Dr. Marcus Warner, p. 118

thoughts come into our mind. In this process, we may realize that we have believed a lie related to the wound. God is able to connect with us on both the slow track and the fast track, and as we move through the elements of relational discipleship, we will become more comfortable with recognizing which thoughts are God's and which thoughts come from us.

The next 4 Cs are slow track solutions.[5] This means that they accomplish the goal and store new information in our brains, but these solutions don't affect the fast track, where our emotional and body experience is stored. We may continue to struggle with emotional reactions and continued poor choices until we also get healing for the fast track.

- **Confess:** Once we realize we believe a lie related to our wound, we confess (agree with God) that we have believed the lie, and that it is indeed untrue. We may be unsure of the truth at this time, but we are willing to acknowledge the lie.

- **Cancel:** Believing a lie can open us up to influence from demonic spirits, so the next step is to cancel their right to influence us with a simple statement: "In the name of Jesus and by His blood, I cancel the right of any demonic spirit to influence my mind and life."

- **Command:** Now that demonic spirits have no right to remain, we simply command them to leave.

- **Commit:** We now choose to commit ourselves to God's truth and ways; we begin the process of rebuilding our thoughts and renewing our minds as stated in Romans 12:2.[6]

Now that we have "cleaned house," aligned ourselves with God's truth, and updated our slow track, we begin the more involved process of updating our fast track. The deep-seated, very rapid thought processes that drive our behavior and can hinder our freedom take more deliberate effort to bring into alignment with God's truth. The following 2 Cs are designed to work with the fast track.

- **Construct:** We must construct a new thought pattern and new choices. Our thought patterns are built by repetition of thought and experience, just as a path through the woods forms when we take the same route repeatedly. In time, the path is clear and can be traveled rapidly. When we have repeatedly followed a certain thought path over time, it becomes almost automatic. It would take effort to walk an untrav-

---

5 | The first three Cs come from Karl Payne's spiritual warfare teaching.

6 | "Do not conform to the pattern of this world, but be transformed by the renewing of your mind. Then you will be able to test and approve what God's will is—his good, pleasing and perfect will." NIV

eled path. In constructing new thought patterns and choices, we must first see an example or hear a story of a new pattern, then gradually begin to more regularly choose the new "path." This is why Jesus told His disciples, "Follow Me."

- **Connect with Community:** Some of you may have read *The Hunger Games* trilogy by Suzanne Collins or seen the movies. After Peeta was brainwashed by The Capitol, he knew he could not trust his mind and turned to Katniss to help him. My heart both broke and sang when he would look at her and say, "True or not true?" God intended us to have friends who will help us know "true or not true."

   Spending time with people who live by the Spirit and with a renewed mind will make constructing a new thought pattern and choice much quicker and more natural. We learn from examples and stories, so sharing our stories in community is powerful—more powerful for change than more information. The combination of scriptural truth with loving community where there is transparency and gentleness with weakness will result in a full experience of the words of Jesus: "...*you will know the truth, and the truth will set you free,*" and "*I am the way and the truth and the life...*"[7]

- **Listening Prayer** together: Connection with God is always a good beginning and end to our "freedom work." After each time we pass through the steps of Confess, Cancel, Command, Commit, Construct, and Community (an ongoing step), it is helpful to reconnect with God and ask Him again what He wants us to know. Sharing what thoughts come to mind with your community (small group, friends, family, Sunday school class, etc.) will help you learn to receive those thoughts which come from God and discard those that come from your wounded self or from the Enemy. True or not true?

PONDER, JOURNAL, AND DISCUSS:

1. In your own life, what are some issues that might qualify as strongholds? (We will not discuss this answer in our group, so feel free to be very honest.) [Examples of strongholds: performance, people pleasing, avoidance, criticism, appearance, over- or under-responsibility, procrastination, reliance on food/diet, co-dependency, any dependence on something other than relationship with God or healthy people to handle emotional pain]

2. What steps have you taken in the past to address these problems/strongholds? Have you found practical freedom? How might the idea of the slow track and fast track of the brain have affected the amount of freedom you have experienced?

---

7 | John 8:32 and 14:6

3. Our Journey Group is a community where we will practice these steps. Begin asking God to bring to mind people in your local community who would be open to meeting occasionally for "freedom work." This can start with one safe friend with whom you meet every few weeks. Allow God to gently and relationally direct this process.

F.I.S.H.

LESSON 3

Walking in Freedom Together

Freedom spreads as we grow our glad-to-be-together joy and learn to walk in forgiveness and maturity with our community.

> Therefore, as God's chosen people, holy and dearly loved, clothe yourselves with compassion, kindness, humility, gentleness and patience. Bear with each other and forgive one another if any of you has a grievance against someone. Forgive as the Lord forgave you. And over all these virtues put on love, which binds them all together in perfect unity. Colossians 3:12-14 NIV

In Lesson 2, we spoke of individual freedom from wounds, lies, vows, and strongholds. Our freedom in Christ is most powerful as it is experienced relationally. In a heart-focused community, we learn to walk in the freedom that arises out of love from a pure heart, a good conscience, and a sincere faith.[1] We are free to live in true joy and love each other transparently and honestly as we grow in relationship with God, learn to forgive from the heart, and grow in spiritual and emotional maturity.

Let's unpack some of the aspects of Walking in Freedom Together:

- True **Joy** can be defined as "a relational experience in which 'someone's glad to be with me,'"[2] which is very different from *happiness*, which might be defined as "things are going well," "my relationship is running smoothly," "my team just won the championship." True joy is a fast-track emotion that gives us capacity to face the difficulties of life and relationships, whereas happiness fades at the first sign of a problem. The fast track of our brain is wired through relationships, while the slow track of the brain is wired with information.

- Our initial foundation of joy is laid in the first years of life as our family delights in our uniqueness. These interactions of joy begin to

---

1 | 1 Timothy 1:15

2 | *Joy Starts Here*, Wilder, Khouri, Coursey, Sutton, p. 4

wire the fast track of our brain. Throughout life, God provides opportunities to repair and build on this foundation as we meet people who have the capacity to love us in our current condition. God is constantly glad to be with us and as we recognize His joy in us, our foundation becomes more solid, and our capacity grows. Nehemiah 8:10 tells us that the joy of the Lord is our strength. We gain strength as we experience this joy. As we internalize this "glad to be with you" joy of the Lord, we experience Hebrews 4:16; we approach His throne of grace with confidence, so that we may receive mercy and find grace to help us in our time of need.

- **Relationship with God** grows as we approach Him with confidence to receive His mercy and grace. Not only do we study the Word in order to know Him, but the Hebrew word often translated "know" is *yada*, which in relation to God is defined as "to have an intimate experiential knowledge of Him."[3] Our study of Scripture intertwines with our experiential knowledge of God to provide a rich relationship, far beyond what either study or experience alone could give. You'll notice that this beautiful mix of Scripture and relational experience with God is providing healthy wiring for both the fast and slow tracks.

- **Forgiveness** is both received and given in a community where "glad to be with you" joy is the norm. From this secure foundation, we learn to restore joy by asking for forgiveness when we are in the wrong and by offering forgiveness when we have been wronged. More mature believers model and guide us through the process of forgiveness. Consider Paul's words in 2 Corinthians 2:7-11:

> "Now instead, you ought to forgive and comfort him, so that he will not be overwhelmed by excessive sorrow. I urge you, therefore, to reaffirm your love for him. Another reason I wrote you was to see if you would stand the test and be obedient in everything. Anyone you forgive, I also forgive. And what I have forgiven—if there was anything to forgive—I have forgiven in the sight of Christ for your sake, in order that Satan might not outwit us. For we are not unaware of his schemes." NIV

Paul knew that sin could not be ignored, but he also knew that Satan could use unforgiveness of the sin just as he used the sin to bring trouble to the body at Corinth. Paul's mature guidance allowed the believers to address the sin among them while still walking in the freedom of forgiving and being forgiven.

---

3 | *Vine's Complete Expository Dictionary*, p. 131

Learning the facts about forgiveness and its necessity is important for the slow track, while adding the relational capacity to walk out the reality of forgiveness is a fast-track skill.

- **Maturity** grows best in heart-focused community where we have models of love, joy, forgiveness, intimacy with God, and other relational skills that enable us to walk in freedom. Notice the community aspect of these verses about maturity:[4]

  > **Ephesians 4:13** "*...we all* reach unity in the faith and in the knowledge of the Son of God and *become mature*, attaining to the whole measure of the fullness of Christ."

  > **Philippians 3:15** "*All of us, then, who are mature* should take such a view of things. And if on some point you think differently, that too God will make clear to you."

  > **Colossians 1:28** "He is the one we proclaim, admonishing and teaching everyone with all wisdom, so that we may present *everyone fully mature* in Christ."

We see that Jesus was establishing a body, a family, a building, a Kingdom in which each person is integral to the growth of the whole. Our freedom in Him is both individual and corporate—our ability to walk in freedom is deeply impacted by our neighbor's freedom. We belong to each other.

PONDER, JOURNAL, AND DISCUSS:

1. Which of these aspects of freedom in community have you experienced: joy, relationship with God, forgiveness, and maturity? How did your community help each other grow in each of these?

2. What difference do you think it would make to a family or community when there is a focus on growing relational capacity and skills as well as acquiring information about living a life of freedom together?

3. Did this lesson bring up any new thoughts or perspectives about joy, relationship with God, forgiveness, or maturity?

---

4 | Scripture references are NIV. Emphasis added.

F.I.S.H.
LSSON 4

Identity in Christ

Therefore, if anyone is in Christ, he is a new creation.
The old has passed away; behold, the new has come.
– 2 Corinthians 5:17 ESV

Heart-focused community grows as we know our identity in Christ and remind each other that this identity is the most true thing about us. Many of us grew up with an identity that came from our family or friends:

Black sheep	Goody goody
Shy and quiet	Suzy Sunshine
Brainy	Chubby
Super Christian	Loudmouth

While these identities may have seemed to fit our personality or actions, they are not what is "most true" about us. We all have a tendency to identify each other based on performance, appearance, temperament, or malfunctions. **God designed us to see ourselves through the eyes of others, and our personal identity (perception of ourselves) is built on the faces we see looking at us and the messages on those faces.** With this thought in mind, consider the blessing God gave the high priests to speak over His people:

"The LORD bless you and keep you; the LORD *make his face shine on you* and be gracious to you; The LORD *lift up his countenance upon you and give you peace.*" Numbers 6:24-26 NIV *emphasis added*

Matthew Henry's Commentary on this verse says that for God's face to shine upon us means "To be under the almighty protection of God our Saviour; to enjoy his favour as the smile of a loving Father, or as the cheering beams of the sun."[1] **God desires for us to receive His smiling face as a foundation of our identity.**

---

1 | www.biblehub.com/commentaries/numbers/6-25.htm

In Christ, we received a new identity. It is important for us to know the "legal" truths of this new identity. See the chart at the end of the lesson for some aspects of this new, true identity as compiled by Neil Anderson of Freedom in Christ Ministries.

As we interact with those people who see us with the eyes of God, who remind us that this new identity is the truest thing about us, we build our new identity as the person God created us to be. As members of a heart-focused community, it is our job to look for the true identity of our family and friends and point it out to them.

How does this work in the nitty gritty of everyday life? As mentioned in our last lesson, experiences of relational joy with family and friends build our capacity to face the difficulties of life and relationships. As our capacity grows, we are more able to receive and live from the reality of our new identity in Christ. We also gain an increased ability to see others as our new creation selves and maintain our "glad to be together" joy even when we are acting out of our old identity.

Looking back at our lessons about Freedom, it is interesting and important to know that wounds, lies, vows, and strongholds have an impact on our ability to live from our identity in Christ. This is why we recommend doing "freedom work" with a few friends on a consistent basis. There may be many issues to address in early freedom sessions, but as time passes and we consistently and promptly deal with our wounds, freedom work will become more like maintenance rather than deep overhaul. The freedom gained will add to our capacity to live from our God-given identity.

The elements of Relational Heart-Focused Discipleship are Freedom, Identity, Walking in the Spirit, and Heart to Heart Community. Rather than viewing these elements as linear steps or building blocks, it might be helpful to view them as points on a spiral—we will engage with these elements over and over as our walk grows deeper with God and our community. Over time, we will learn how to live from our true identity in a growing variety of increasingly complex situations.

> Ephesians 4:13: "...*we all* reach unity in the faith and in the knowledge of the Son of God and *become mature*, attaining to the whole measure of the fullness of Christ." NIV

PONDER, JOURNAL, AND DISCUSS:

1. What are some of the identities you have experienced in your life, whether at home, church, school, work, or with friends? How have these identities worked to your benefit? To your detriment? Did these identities come from your performance, appearance, temperament, malfunctions, or something else? Prayerfully consider: Are there lies you have believed based on these identities?

2. Prayerfully read through the "Who I Am in Christ" statements and see what statements are highlighted to you.

    Journal: "What feels important about this particular statement? God, is there something you want me to know about this statement?" Write a prayer of appreciation for how this statement applies to you.

3. Are there times when you do see yourself as your new creation self? What characterizes these times? Do you still find yourself basing your identity on performance, appearance, temperament, or malfunctions? Write a few words that would describe a life where you remembered your own identity in Christ and also saw other people as their true identity.

Freedom & Identity Exercise

Read the following identity statements out loud.

I AM ACCEPTED...

John 1:12	I am God's child.
John 15:15	As a disciple, I am a friend of Jesus Christ.
Romans 5:1	I have been justified (declared righteous).
1 Corinthians 6:17	I am united with the Lord, and I am one with Him in spirit.
1 Corinthians 6:19-20	I have been bought with a price and I belong to God.
1 Corinthians 12:27	I am a member of Christ's body.
Ephesians 1:3-8	I have been chosen by God and adopted as His child.
Colossians 1:13-14	I have been redeemed and forgiven of all my sins.
Colossians 2:9-10	I am complete in Christ.
Hebrews 4:14-16	I have direct access to the throne of grace through Jesus Christ.

I AM SECURE...

Romans 8:1-2	I am free from condemnation.
Romans 8:28	I am assured that God works for my good in all circumstances.
Romans 8:31-39	I am free from any condemnation brought against me and I cannot be separated from the love of God.
2 Corinthians 1:21-22	I have been established, anointed, and sealed by God.
Colossians 3:1-4	I am hidden with Christ in God.
Philippians 1:6	I am confident that God will complete the good work He started in me.

Philippians 3:20	I am a citizen of heaven.
2 Timothy 1:7	I have not been given a spirit of fear but of power, love, and a sound mind.
1 John 5:18	I am born of God and the evil one cannot touch me.
John 15:5	I am a branch of Jesus Christ, the true vine, and a channel of His life.
John 15:16	I have been chosen and appointed to bear fruit.
1 Corinthians 3:16	I am God's temple.
2 Corinthians 5:17-21	I am a minister of reconciliation for God.
Ephesians 2:6	I am seated with Jesus Christ in the heavenly realm.
Ephesians 2:10	I am God's workmanship.
Ephesians 3:12	I may approach God with freedom and confidence.
Philippians 4:13	I can do all things through Christ, who strengthens me.

1. Note which statements feel true to you and which do not.

2. Taking one statement which feels untrue, ask God to reveal any wounds you have suffered or lies you may have believed that would cause this statement to feel untrue to you.

3. As thoughts come to you, make note of them and share them with the group.

4. Take turns following the freedom sequence of "Confess, Cancel, Command, Commit, and Construct" together. (Refer to Lesson 2 to refresh your memory of this sequence.)

5. Spend some time speaking the identity statements to each other, particularly emphasizing those that felt untrue.

6. Over the next weeks, notice when thoughts occur to you that are not in alignment with the identity statements and spend time with God, asking Him to confirm your identity in Him.

7. Call a group member when troubling thoughts occur. Remember, God created us to build our identities in community!

LESSON 5

Growing into My Identity

Therefore, if anyone is in Christ, he is a new creation.
The old has passed away; behold, the new has come.
– 2 Corinthians 5:17 ESV

As we experience Jesus together, our way of life begins to match our identity. We grow in Christlikeness. Growing into our identity in Christ is a community effort—God designed us to grow the identity that is reflected to us by Him and "our people," those whose see us from His perspective as new creations growing into maturity. This brings to mind the Scripture 1 Corinthians 13:12-13 ESV: "For now we see in a mirror dimly, but then face to face. Now I know in part; then I shall know fully, even as I have been fully known. So now faith, hope, and love abide, these three; but the greatest of these is love." The more we see ourselves reflected in the mirror of God's face and His mature people, the more fully we will exhibit Christlikeness.

Our part in this beautiful dance of growing identity is twofold: giving and receiving. We receive God's truth from His word and from time spent with Him; we receive from our brothers and sisters in Christ who see us from His perspective; we give by sharing His truth with others and by letting them know we see them as He does. As we are fully known for our true identity in Him, we are enabled tosee others in this same way—believers on a path to see God and themselves ever more clearly. What a difference it makes when we see each other this way.

It's helpful to notice that Jesus had a closer relationship with the Twelve than with His other followers and didn't rely on the synagogue to be His place of deep fellowship. We can follow His example by looking for a few brothers or sisters in Christ with whom to develop this deeper relationship of heart-focused discipleship. As we grow in our ability to see each other through God's eyes and to encourage each other in our true identity, it's possible that others from our church or community will want to join us. Don't be afraid to start with just one other person to grow in freedom and identity!

One way to combine freedom and identity work is to meet with one or two friends and review the "Who I Am in Christ" list from Lesson 4 together. Note which statements feel "true" to you and which do not. Together, pray and ask God to reveal to you any wounds you may have suffered or lies you may have believed that have affected your ability to believe and receive these identity statements. As thoughts come to you, make note of them and share them with the group. Take turns following the freedom sequence of "Confess, Cancel, Command, Commit, and Construct" together. Finally, spend some time speaking the identity statements to each other, particularly emphasizing those that felt untrue. Over the next weeks, notice when thoughts occur to you that are not in alignment with the identity statements and spend time with God, asking Him to confirm your identity in Him. It's also a good idea to call a group member when troubling thoughts occur so that you have help with the "Construct" and "Connect/Community" freedom components. An outline of this process is attached as an Addendum to this lesson.

As we all grow into the freedom of living from our true identity in Christ, we will notice that God has gifted us each with different aspects of His personality in order to equip us for the particular situations He knows we will face. Look at Ephesians 2:10 from the Amplified Bible:

> "For we are His workmanship [His own master work, a work of art], created in Christ Jesus [reborn from above—spiritually transformed, renewed, ready to be used] for good works, which God prepared [for us] beforehand [taking paths which He set], so that we would walk in them [living the good life which He prearranged and made ready for us]."

Discovering our individual identity in Christ is another ongoing task of discipleship. Not only have we been restored to relationship with God and become joint heirs with Christ, we are also now part of God's plan to expand His Kingdom on the earth. We are His work of art (or poetry, as the word "workmanship" is sometimes translated), and we express His personality, thoughts, and plans to the world around us.

As we come to know one another deeply we begin to notice these particular heart characteristics and gifts that God has placed within us and others. All God's people are called to be loving, for instance, but some of us express His love through hospitality, others through affection, through including the forgotten, welcoming newcomers, working toward social justice, or through many other creative expressions of God's love. In the same way, there are many expressions of justice, mercy, kindness, faithfulness, patience, or the other myriad characteristics of our Father. We will talk more about this in later lessons but begin to look for and comment on the ways in which you and others express God's characteristics in everyday life. We each have a special "flavor" of God to express to our world, and recognizing this "flavor" in each other builds joy between us and gratitude toward our creative God.

PONDER, JOURNAL, AND DISCUSS:

1. What have you noticed about the difference in your "head knowledge" (slow track) of your identity in Christ and your "heart knowledge" or experience (fast track)? When life is difficult, which of these tends to rule your thinking? When we notice that our immediate response to a situation is aligned with our identity in Christ, it means that both our slow and fast tracks have received and believed the message!

2. What experiences have you had of "receiving" your identity in Christ from other believers? What about "giving"—telling others their identity in Him?

3. As you think of yourself as God's work of art to express His personality to the world, what characteristics come to mind? If this question is difficult for you, another way of approaching this concept is to think of which characteristics of God are especially meaningful to you. Write down a few of the characteristics you appreciate about God and any of His characteristics you see in yourself.

4. See if you can schedule a time to go through the Freedom and Identity Exercise with a friend or two, and notice what you learn about yourself.

LESSON 6

Walking by the Spirit: Tuning In

> But the Helper, the Holy Spirit, whom the Father will send in my name, he will teach you all things and bring to your remembrance all that I have said to you. — John 14:26 ESV

Jesus promised us that the Holy Spirit will be our teacher and advocate. Walking by the Spirit means listening to Jesus as a way of life. Just as our freedom and identity in Christ are established at salvation but take some time and effort to understand and experience in our daily lives, walking in the Spirit is a way of life that is available to us immediately as Christians but often seems elusive or inaccessible.

What are the "brass tacks" of walking by the Spirit? Are there practical steps to take for such a heavenly activity? In his book *Toward a Deeper Walk*, Dr. Marcus Warner provides some guidance that comes from his own time of wrestling with this issue.

In order to walk by the Spirit, we must SLOW down our daily pace, so it's appropriate that the key ideas of walking by the Spirit spell this word:

Seek God

Listen to God

Obey God

Watch God and the enemy

Seek God. God can be intimately known, and we must seek Him in order to build that relationship. In Lesson 2 of Jumpstart, we learned that *appreciation* prepares our brains for relational interactions, and this is particularly true of our relationship with God. Psalm 95:2 tells us we can come into His presence with thanksgiving. As we focus on what we appreciate about God and His gifts to us, we can become more aware of His presence with us. Begin your time with God with several minutes of focused attention on specific appreciation memories—times when you knew He was with you, or when you felt peaceful or joyful. This time of appreciation will help warm up your mind to enter His presence.

We can seek God through *reading the Word* and asking for His perspective on what we are reading, noticing what thoughts bubble to the surface. For centuries believers with an intimate relationship with God have made it their habit to spend time in Scripture accompanied by journaling their thoughts. Humbly sharing our journaling with friends who walk with God provides a safety net to ensure what we are sensing is congruent with the heart and Word of God.

Music is another powerful tool to use in seeking God. Because our sense of hearing is so closely tied to bonding, it's helpful to listen to and sing music that has been part of our experiences with God in the past. Our mind and emotions return to that place of connection, and we can more easily sense Him again. The more frequently we listen to music that brings a sense of peace and joy, the wider our "library" of God-connection music becomes.

Setting aside time to notice God's *creation* is often an open door into God's presence. Whether we go hiking in a remote location full of grandeur or simply stop to look closely at a flower growing next to the sidewalk, these moments of noticing what has been created by God bring us back to Him. Consider placing a live plant in your office or taking a walk at lunch—whatever it takes, connect with creation and you will find connection with the Creator.

Listen to God. Because God speaks in the still small voice which is most often heard in our own thoughts, listening to God has been the source of much confusion through the years. Adding to the differences in ability and desire to hear from God individually are family and church teachings, relational styles, personality types, and life experiences.

As we combine the tools of appreciation, reading the Word, music, and spending time in nature with building humble, transparent, heart-focused community, our recognition of God's voice will begin to grow. God's voice will increase our appreciation, peace, and love for people, and it will always be consistent with Scripture.

Listening to God will lead into joyful **Obedience.** Psalm 37:4 ESV, "Delight yourself in the LORD, and he will give you the desires of your heart." As we seek God and listen to Him, our minds and desires begin to align with His thoughts. Obedience becomes a joy as we walk in step with our Savior and Friend, and even in those times when our obedience is less than joyful, we can trust that our thoughts and actions will begin to rhyme with His as we continually delight ourselves in Him.

Enjoy again this quote from *Joyful Journey* which was first introduced in our Listening to Jesus lesson:

> In Ephesians 2:10, Paul uses the Greek word *poiema*, which literally means God's poetry. When *poiema* is translated "handiwork" or "workmanship" it misses the following important point. Poetry in scripture does not rhyme sounds; it follows the Hebrew pattern and rhymes thoughts. This means that as God's poetry, our thoughts can rhyme with our Heavenly Father's. That is amazing! How can it work? We know that as we become intimate with someone, we begin to finish each other's sentences and thoughts. In a deep, authentic, mutual-mind state, we actually don't know where our thoughts stop and the other person's thoughts begin. This is exactly what can happen between God and us too. *A mutual-mind state with God results in an emulation of His character and heart; we are showing the world the poet behind the poetry.* As our mutual-mind state becomes stronger, we are able to live out our purpose of being created for good works."[1]

Watching God is an extension of our joyful obedience. We see this in the life of Joshua, who learned to seek and listen to God in the tent of meeting with Moses. Exodus 33:11 tells us that even when Moses left the tent after his times of listening to God, Joshua stayed behind. Joshua went into the land of Canaan to spy out what God had given Israel, and only Joshua and Caleb were ready to trust and watch God give them the land. Moses passed leadership of the Israelites to Joshua, and in *Toward a Deeper Walk*, Marcus Warner points out how Joshua learned that seeking, listening, obeying, and watching was the formula for success, and moving without this relational connection to God brought failure and disaster.

Another command to watch was given to us by Jesus in Matthew 26:41, "watch and pray so you do not fall into temptation." Much like the Israelites in Joshua's time, when we lose sight of our relational connection to the Father, our enemy steps in to create trouble. Strangely enough, keeping our eyes firmly fixed on Jesus enables us also to see and avoid the traps of the enemy.

In *Toward a Deeper Walk*, Marcus tells us,

> "'Watch and pray' Jesus said, 'so you do not fall into temptation' (Matthew 26:41). "Be alert and sober-minded,' wrote Peter 'for your adversary the devil prowls around like a roaring lion, seeking someone to destroy' (1 Peter 5:8). Peter knew something about this. He had not listened to Jesus in the Garden of Gethsemane when he was told to watch and pray,

---

1 | *Joyful Journey*, p. 3

thus he was not ready for the enemy attack... Satan had been granted special permission to attack Peter as a means of testing him. Peter failed the test, but that is not the end of the story. Satan wanted to sift Peter in order to destroy him. God allowed the sifting because He knew He could use it in Peter's life and overcome it in the end. God's sovereignty is such that by the time He was done with Peter, all Satan had accomplished by his attack was to help God make Peter into an even more formidable opponent... Peter learned the importance of being alert and sober minded. He learned to watch and pray."[2]

PONDER, JOURNAL, AND DISCUSS:

1. As you meditate on the elements **Seek, Listen, Obey,** and **Watch,** which of these seems to come most easily to you in your daily walk with God? Ask Him what has made this element easier for you. Ask Him what He would have you do to grow in the other elements.

2. As you read the quote about having a mutual mind state from *Joyful Journey,* can you think of a person or two with whom you have this mutual mind? How did this occur—how much time have you spent with this person, what type of conversations have you had, what interests do you share? How could you apply these ideas to your relationship with God so that your thoughts begin to "rhyme" more with His thoughts?

3. Can you think of times in your life where your relational connection with God enabled you to see and avoid the temptations and traps of Satan? Write out an appreciation memory about one of these times and add it to your appreciation list.

---

2 | *Toward a Deeper Walk,* pp. 143-144

F.I.S.H.

LESSON 7

Walking by the Spirit: Community, Power, & Authority

The Holy Spirit enables us to discern truth from counterfeit. Walking by the Spirit gives us comfort, guidance, and courage, as well as authority and power as He chooses.

Reading through the New Testament references to the Holy Spirit makes it clear that it is in and through the Spirit that we discern God's truth from the many counterfeits of the world. The Spirit is our Helper—the Spirit of truth, the Spirit of love, joy, peace, glory, and hope who is contrasted to law, flesh, death, fear, evil, deceit, error, human tradition, dead works, and divisions.[1]

Lesson 6 encouraged us to Seek, Listen, Obey, and Watch as a guide to walking in the Spirit. The component of *watching* referred to watching both God and the enemy. When we hear of all the counterfeits that are offered by the world and the enemy, we realize how important it is to truly know our Father through His Spirit.

An incident from my brother's life illustrates the importance of intimately knowing our Father's voice. My brother Bruce wore a thick beard for many years—neither his wife nor his children had ever seen him without it. Without telling his family of his plans, Bruce shaved off his beard one morning and went to work. After work, he pulled into the parking lot at the local grocery store and realized his wife Ellen and their children were parked next to him and getting out of their car. Bruce stepped out of his car and looked his wife in the eyes and said, "Hey there, good looking!" Ellen gave him a haughty look of disdain and quickly reached for the children. However, the children were facing away from Bruce when he spoke and knew this was the voice of their much-loved father. As Ellen attempted to hustle them away from this strange, flirtatious man, she was horrified to see them running to him and jumping into his arms! Regardless of appearances, they knew their father's voice! We, too, can learn to recognize our Father's voice even in confusing and distressing situations.

---

1 | www.biblegateway.com, search for "Spirit."

Having companions with us as we learn and practice the skills of seeking, listening, obeying, and watching provides a safety net for those times when we are vulnerable to counterfeits due to wounds, lies, strongholds, lack of experience, inattention, or fatigue. The Word + the Spirit + the Body is a powerful combination. A protective community provides an environment where we can practice listening together, humbly sharing what we receive and notice, clarifying what might be counterfeit and what is true, and learning how to reduce the effect of the counterfeit in our lives.

What does it mean to "reduce the effect of the counterfeit in our lives"? Our enemy is the Father of Lies, so he will continually seek to deceive us into accepting counterfeits of God's gifts. We can't prevent his counterfeits and deceit coming our way, but we can calmly deal with them and continue to live in joy and peace. Just as my niece and nephew immediately recognized their father by his voice and would not run to another man, we can learn to know our Father so well that we quickly recognize and renounce the counterfeits that will be offered to us in our lives.

Counteracting counterfeits in our lives will likely occur as both "event" and "process." For instance, going through *The Steps to Freedom in Christ*[2] is a helpful tool for renouncing and removing counterfeits that may be impacting your ability to connect deeply with God. Other events might include REAL[3] prayer or Immanuel Prayer[4] sessions, breakthroughs from the Word, conversations with friends, or worship experiences. These are concrete times in which we recognize that we have made substantial progress or regained ground that had been surrendered to the enemy.

Because renewing the mind (rewiring the fast track of the brain) occurs over time and through repetition, much of our growth in recognizing the difference between God's voice and the enemy's counterfeits will happen as a process. Practicing community with both more and less experienced Christians provides the opportunity for us to learn from the more experienced believers, practice with our peers, and model for and teach those less experienced than us. Learning about the power and authority we have in Christ with truly mature believers modeling the gentleness, joy, peace, and hope that comes from walking by the Spirit helps prevent misuse of power and authority. When emotional and spiritual maturity are included as goals, the community will produce protectors who use power and authority in Christlike ways.

---

2 | We recommend that you go through *The Steps to Freedom in Christ* during Unit 5, "Living by the Spirit." Deeper Walk has a list of trained facilitators to whom we will refer you.

3 | *Understanding the Wounded Heart*, pp. 60-63, Dr. Marcus Warner. Also, find a free download of the REAL Prayer handout at Deeper Walk bookstore.

4 | Immanuel Prayer was developed by Dr. Karl Lehman, and training is also available through Alive & Well.

What authority do we have as believers? In Christ, we have authority over the work of the enemy as it affects us and those who come to us for help. As Dr. Warner states in *What Every Believer Should Know About Spiritual Warfare*, "In Ephesians 2:6 we read that God raised us up together with Christ and seated us together with Him in heavenly places. From this position at the right hand of the Father we have intimacy with God and authority over the enemy. We no longer struggle as victims, but we wage war as victors."[5]

Praying the Scriptures is a beautiful, powerful tool of authority, particularly when combined with listening prayer. As we read the Word, God may highlight certain phrases or verses that can be prayed for ourselves or others, and as we listen to God, we may sense His guidance toward other Scriptures. Intercession which combines the authority of Scripture with the intimacy of relationship has incredible depth and power, especially when practiced in community.

As we grow our intimacy with God and awareness of His constant presence with us, we listen closely to Him for guidance in how to exercise our authority as believers. We learn tools for spiritual warfare not so that we can strike out to fight Satan alone, but so that we recognize God's provision for each individual situation. Additionally, our community of practice provides support and guidance as we learn to walk in our authority.

Our next unit will examine ways to build this community of practice—a heart-focused community where we can create belonging, build secure relationships and listen to Jesus together as a way of life.

PONDER, JOURNAL, AND DISCUSS:

1. Can you think of some "events" in your life where you saw specific progress or breakthrough in your spiritual life? List as many of these as possible. These events would be excellent appreciation memories to add to your Appreciation Library.

2. What value can you see in having a "community of practice" in which there are Christians who are upstream from you in spiritual maturity, peers with you, and downstream from you? Sometimes such a community begins with two people who begin meeting to practice Check In and Listening to Jesus together. Ask God for such a partner and see what thoughts surface!

3. This week try an experiment in praying Scripture. Each day read Ephesians 1 and see what God highlights for you to pray for yourself and others. Journal these prayers.

---

5 | *What Every Believer Should Know About Spiritual Warfare*, 2nd Edition, p. 33.

maturity matters
UNIT FOUR

LESSON 1

Introduction to Maturity

"Maturity is about reaching one's God-given potential. It means maximizing our skills and talents, and using them effectively, while growing into the full capability of our individual designs."[1]

The foundation for maturity is our ability to sustain the rhythms of joy and quiet. In a healthy community, the pathway toward maturity will lead to an ever-increasing ability to sustain these rhythms in complex and difficult situations. Newborns have no capacity to build joy or to quiet themselves, but within a year, these skills begin to emerge through their interactions with family members. Young children are often able to sustain joy and quiet themselves in a limited range of situations, but these skills may quickly drop when challenges arise. Through the teen years and into adulthood, we will ideally see rhythms of joy and quiet become quite consistent, and other maturity tasks are added so that joyful, peaceful adults are launched into the world with capacity to face life's challenges in a satisfying, stable way, adding their own personal flair and gifts to society.

A person without this foundation of joy and quiet may function fairly well while living at home, and even in the initial launch into independent life. Eventually, however, life's wear and tear will reveal the faulty construction, and the painful process of collapsing begins. A person without a firm joy and quiet foundation cannot withstand the stress of breakups or losses, nor survive the pressure of growth and maturity. Because this foundation is needed to help us manage difficult emotions, we may notice a gradual turn to BEEPS (behaviors, events, experiences, people, and substances)[2] to avoid or mask emotional pain and create a false sense of joy and quiet. Increased usage of BEEPS is frequently seen when a person with low joy strength (capacity) suffers losses or failure. We've seen (or perhaps experienced) the crash and burn that sometimes happens as the complexities of life multiply.

---

1 | *Living from the Heart Jesus Gave You*, p. 33.

2 | Ed Khouri created this memory device.

How can we obtain this strong foundation if we didn't receive it in child-hood, and how can we prevent or repair the damage from the "crash and burn" we or others may have experienced? What are the skills and tasks we need to reach the level of maturity that is appropriate for our chronological age?

There is very good news for those of us with serious maturity gaps! While most of the brain stops growing at certain stages of development, the brain's "joy center," located in the right orbital prefrontal cortex, is the only section of the brain that never loses its capacity to grow! It grows in response to real, joy-filled relationships.[3]

The Maturity Stages we will discuss in this unit are:

- Infant (Birth to age 4)
- Child (Age 4 through 12)
- Adult (Age 13 to birth of first child)
- Parent (Birth of first child)
- Elder (Last child reaches adulthood)

Infant Maturity

The most important tasks in infant maturity are building strong, loving bonds with both parents (or another male and female) and receiving from others who give joyfully. At infant maturity, we need others to love and care for us sacrificially. We bond well when those around us practice the rhythms of joy and quiet—interacting with us at our capacity, meeting our needs without expectation that we will meet the needs of others. As this occurs, we develop a strong, joyful identity. As we move through the infant stage and begin to approach the child stage, we begin to notice that others also have needs, and we want to begin to take care of ourselves.

Child Maturity

Learning to take care of ourselves is a key task during child maturity. Rather than being cared for without expectations, we begin to ask for what we need, make ourselves understandable, and develop our personality, talents, and resources into a strong individual identity. We learn what is satisfying to us personally and become self-directed; one child may enjoy running fast and climbing trees, while another may find satisfaction in books, artwork, or science experiments. Life is not all about personal satisfaction, however; child maturity also involves learning how to do hard things, even ones we don't feel like doing. As adults in our lives allow us to try different activities, come alongside us in difficult chores, and tell us the story of our family and our people, we begin to see how we fit into our world, and become eager to expand our horizons.

---

3 | *Living from the Heart Jesus Gave You*, p. 35

Adult Maturity

Adult maturity can begin at the time of puberty if child maturity is well-established. At puberty, hormonal changes create a sense of disequilibrium that disrupts our individual identity, and this propels us into a search for "our people." If the child tasks of doing hard things and knowing who we are and what is personally satisfying aren't in place, we may gravitate toward groups that give us immediate gratification or that provide a group identity that doesn't encourage self-expression or the adult maturity task of satisfaction for self *and* others. Learning to care for self plus one, to find solutions that are fair to us and others, to allow others to be themselves while we remain ourselves, these are tasks for a mature adult. When an adult becomes adept at navigating life with all these tasks in place, he or she may be ready for marriage. Without solid adult maturity, marriage is likely to more resemble a tug of war than a joyful, peaceful walk together.

Parent Maturity

It's an unfortunate fact that modern culture provides little support for our journey down the maturity pathway; in fact, it's a rare community that is aware of the maturity tasks needed at each stage. This means that most of us become parents well before we attain parent maturity. In adult maturity, we are able to take care of self plus one in a mutually satisfying way. Parent maturity can give sacrificially and joyfully to take care of children who are unable to consistently provide anything in return other than gummy smiles, sticky hugs, plenty of messes, and sleepless nights. Children learn that they have value simply because they exist, and parents represent the character of God to their children. This opportunity to represent the everlasting, unrelenting, sacrificial love of our Father is one of life's great honors.

Aunts, uncles, and friends who have no children can challenge themselves to step in and give sacrificially as well. What a gift to parents when mature friends and family stand in the gap to give children more role models, laps to sit in, trips to the zoo, and maybe a nap or two for Mom and Dad. Extended family and friends provide the village needed to raise a child.

Elder Maturity

Once our last child has entered Adult Maturity (around age 13), we are chronologically ready for elder maturity, which means that we extend our sacrificial, joyful giving to our community. Since we've already given our time and capacity to our family in order to bring the children to adult maturity, we are prepared to care for others without falling into codependency or other fear bonds. It would be hard to overestimate the value of true elders in a community.

PONDER, JOURNAL, AND DISCUSS:

1. Ask Jesus to bring an appreciation memory to your mind. Spend three minutes fully entering into that memory. Move to question 2.

2. Review the Infant and Child Maturity Checklist at the end of this lesson. Note which of these tasks you have completed and which are incomplete. Note your strengths and any weaknesses or gaps you notice.

3. Reconnect with Immanuel and ask Him, "How do you see me today? What do you want me to know about maturity?" If you are feeling inadequate or struggling with pain, share this pain with Jesus, particularly journaling or talking with Him about what makes you sad about this situation. After you share with Him, ask Him, "What makes you sad about this situation? How do you want to be with me in my sadness?"

Infant Stage[4]

☐ I have experienced strong, loving, caring bonds with mother/a woman.

☐ I have experienced strong, loving, caring bonds with father/a man.

☐ Important needs were met until I learned to ask.

☐ Others took the lead and synchronized with me and my feelings first.

☐ Quiet together times helped me calm myself with people around.

☐ Important people have seen me through the "eyes of heaven."

☐ I can both receive and give life.

☐ I receive with joy and without guilt or shame.

☐ I can now synchronize with others and their feelings.

☐ I found people to imitate so that I now have a personality I like.

☐ I learned to regulate and quiet the "big six" emotions.

    o Anger
    o Fear
    o Sadness
    o Disgust
    o Shame
    o Hopeless despair

☐ I can return to joy from every emotion and restore broken relationships.

☐ I stay the same person over time.

☐ I know how to rest.

---

4 | from E. James Wider, *Living With Men*

Child Stage

- ☐ I can do things I don't feel like doing.
- ☐ I can do hard things (even if they cause me some pain).
- ☐ I can separate my feelings, my imagination, and reality in my relationships.
- ☐ I am comfortable with reasonable risks, attempts, and failures.
- ☐ I have received love I did not have to earn.
- ☐ I know how my family came to be the way it is—family history.
- ☐ I know how God's family came to be the way it is.
- ☐ I know the "big picture" of life with the stages of maturity.
- ☐ I can take care of myself.
- ☐ I ask for what I need.
- ☐ I enjoy self-expression.
- ☐ I am growing in the things I am good at doing (personal resources and talents).
- ☐ I help other people to understand me better if they don't respond well to me.
- ☐ I have learned to control my cravings.
- ☐ I know what satisfies me.
- ☐ I see myself through the "eyes of heaven."

LESSON 2

Infant, Child, & Transitions

All of us will likely find gaps in our maturity in the Infant and Child Maturity levels. No parent or community is perfect, and our society has become busier and more mobile than ever, and neighbors are unlikely to know each other closely. This prevents the village from raising the children, which is done by providing a wide range of brain skills for a child to learn from a variety of family members and friends. Fortunately, our brain's chemistry retains the ability to grow and change throughout life.

It is very common to feel frustration, sadness, shame, or even humiliation upon reading through the Infant and Child Maturity Checklist. We may realize that we missed out on some important tasks and are not as mature as our age would indicate. Hold on to your hope!

If we don't have a community around us, we can acquire new skills and complete maturity tasks by joining in multigenerational groups in our church, volunteer, or learning organizations. I've known people who found multigenerational community in knitting groups, book clubs, on mission trips, in community projects, or other unexpected places.

The most important task in Infant maturity is to learn to receive from others. When this task is missing, we may find ourselves at one of two extremes, or a third in-between spot:

1. We may not be able to receive from others, feeling obligated to give rather than receive. This often leads to resentment, as we are created by God to *receive* as well as to give. We can learn to receive well by letting people know what we'd like, by receiving compliments with a simple "thank you," and by receiving help or service from those around us when offered. A failure to receive not only leaves us stalled in immaturity, but it also blocks others from experiencing the delight of giving.

2. We may constantly be trying to get other people to take care of us, refusing to grow past this stage of receiving without the need for giving

in return. This often gives rise to resentment in those around us, as we are self-centered and refuse to take responsibility for our part of the load of life. When we realize we are in this state, we can ask others to remind us to do our share of the work, and give those close to us permission to refuse to do things for us that we should be doing for ourselves.

3. The third "in-between" spot we may occupy when we don't learn to or have the opportunity to receive well is passive-aggressive behavior. We might hint at what we'd like others to do, but then refuse to allow them to help us. We might say we don't need anything, but then become subtly or openly angry when nothing is given. This is similar to situation 1 above, and both can result from parents who don't know how to give what we need, or from being what is called a parentified child—a child who has to care for his or her parents rather than being cared for by them. Growth in this area occurs as we let people close to us know that they can gently point out to us when we are doing these behaviors, and we can practice asking for what we need and like in various situations.

The major task of Child Maturity is taking care of oneself. This task flows naturally when we have spent our infant years (from birth to 4th birthday) receiving without the need to give, along with the other Infant Maturity tasks. As well-nurtured children approach their fourth birthday, they begin to demand that they can do things for themselves.

In *Living from the Heart Jesus Gave You*, it is observed that as we move through the maturity stages, transitions can be difficult in a predictable way. As we enter a maturity stage, we are clunky and awkward at the skills, and we often turn to others for help. Over time, the skills become more automatic (less conscious) and we fluidly walk through our day, utilizing the skills with ease. Over time, tension builds as we begin to feel a natural desire to move forward into the next stage of maturity. This may be most easily seen in the transition between the child and adult phases—one moment an 11-year-old girl is happily playing with dolls, and later the same day she is offering to help her mother cook dinner, mixing up biscuits with surprising skill. If her identity has been formed around joy, her family will enjoy her childlikeness as well as her new maturity.[1]

This transformation cycle can take place periodically throughout life, and is often accompanied by anxiety, depression, or other new feelings. Transformations can follow healing or can take place during the completion of a normal maturity stage. Transformation gives a person a new identity when the old one is broken or too small. As the cycle is completed, a more fully developed self emerges, life skills increase, and so does joy. However, if our

---

1 | *Living from the Heart Jesus Gave You*, pp. 43-47.

awkward transitions are not welcomed with joy and encouragement, we may "stall" our maturity and miss out on important skills. As we seek to replace these skills, it is important that we build our joy strength and capacity by spending time with people who are glad to be with us as we fill our gaps and move on to new maturity.

PONDER, JOURNAL, AND DISCUSS:

1. An infant's primary need is to receive, and if this need is not met, "we spend the rest of our lives trying to get others to take care of us." What might this maturity gap look like in adults who did not receive what they needed? What are some examples of the behaviors of "child adults" who can only take care of themselves, often at the expense of others?[2]

2. Asking people who are above us in maturity to help identify the maturity tasks that we have not yet completed can propel us to our next level. Who can you ask to help you with this?[3]

3. Review the Infant and Child portions of The Life Model: Maturity Indicators in the appendices. Be prepared to discuss what you notice.

Infant Stage

- ☐ I have experienced strong, loving, caring bonds with mother/a woman.
- ☐ I have experienced strong, loving, caring bonds with father/a man.
- ☐ Important needs were met until I learned to ask.
- ☐ Others took the lead and synchronized with me and my feelings first.
- ☐ Quiet together times helped me calm myself with people around.
- ☐ Important people have seen me through the "eyes of heaven."
- ☐ I can both receive and give life.
- ☐ I receive with joy and without guilt or shame.
- ☐ I can now synchronize with others and their feelings.
- ☐ I found people to imitate so that I now have a personality I like.
- ☐ I learned to regulate and quiet the "big six" emotions.
  - o Anger
  - o Fear
  - o Sadness
  - o Disgust
  - o Shame
  - o Hopeless despair

---

2 | *Living from the Heart Jesus Gave You*, pp. 36-39.

3 | Ibid., pp. 43-44.

- [ ] I can return to joy from every emotion and restore broken relationships.
- [ ] I stay the same person over time.
- [ ] I know how to rest.

Child Stage

- [ ] I can do things I don't feel like doing.
- [ ] I can do hard things (even if they cause me some pain).
- [ ] I can separate my feelings, my imagination, and reality in my relationships.
- [ ] I am comfortable with reasonable risks, attempts, and failures.
- [ ] I have received love I did not have to earn.
- [ ] I know how my family came to be the way it is—family history.
- [ ] I know how God's family came to be the way it is.
- [ ] I know the "big picture" of life with the stages of maturity.
- [ ] I can take care of myself.
- [ ] I ask for what I need.
- [ ] I enjoy self-expression.
- [ ] I am growing in the things I am good at doing (personal resources and talents).
- [ ] I help other people to understand me better if they don't respond well to me.
- [ ] I have learned to control my cravings.
- [ ] I know what satisfies me.
- [ ] I see myself through the "eyes of heaven."

LESSON 3

Adult Maturity: RARE

As we've looked at the Maturity Indicators Chart, we see that maturation requires two elements: 1) the individual completes the maturity tasks (the first column) and 2) the family and community provide whatever is necessary for maturation (the middle column) The chart illustrates quite dramatically just how interdependent people are in the maturation process. When family and community fail, a deficit will show up in the middle column, and a "Type A" trauma (the absence of something necessary for growth) is the direct result. The chart clarifies how trauma recovery is related to maturity, and how it is dependent on particular kinds of input from family and community. Persons cannot become prepared to give life unless they first receive it.

People have a God-given, inner desire to increase their maturity so they will be able to live from their hearts. Maturity is often blocked, however, and the blocks usually come from absences in the other two areas—from unfinished trauma recovery and from the lack of life-giving relationships.

Focusing on our gaps in maturity can lead to depression and discouragement. However, the book *Rare Leadership* by Marcus Warner and Jim Wilder provides a positive picture of healthy adult maturity, using the acrostic "RARE."

Remain relational

Act like your Christ self

Return to joy in negative emotions

Endure hardship well

What do these short statements mean, and how on earth do we do them? Remember that Life Model Works has created a *model* of how life works when we are fully mature, fully able to live as the person God created us to be.

Growing into these statements is a lifelong task, not something that we accomplish with an afternoon of prayer and Bible study, or an inner healing prayer appointment. What do these statements mean, and how can we accelerate our growth in these areas?

<u>Remain relational</u>. This is JOB ONE! Keep yourself in relational mode, so that you are able to stay connected and concerned about the people involved in your situation. Relational circuits on = relational mode.

<u>Act like your Christ self</u>. Who did God create you to be? How do you behave as that person in this situation? In John 5:19, Jesus provided us a model when He said, "I only do what I see the Father doing." Staying in intimate contact with Immanuel[1] is the pathway to acting like your Christ self.

<u>Return to joy in negative emotions</u>. Return to your relational self when you experience negative emotion, and also remain relational when you're with someone who is in the midst of negative emotions.

<u>Endure hardship well</u>. Stay relational while in difficult situations, so that you have access to the most creative, problem solving, peaceful part of your brain. Having the maturity to remain stable in ongoing difficulties is important.

Rare Leadership sets forth three practices that will enable you and your people to live out the RARE practices, which will create an emotionally mature community.

3 PRACTICES TO BUILD A RARE COMMUNITY:

1. **Build an Identity Group** ("My People"), which becomes your practice field for RARE skills. This is not necessarily a formal group, but is characterized as follows:

   • A group that develops a healthy atmosphere of failure

     ◦ It's okay to fail here.

     ◦ We are still glad to be with you!

     ◦ Failure is the first step to success.

   • Members who help you discover who God created you to be

   • Members who help you remember who God created you to be

   • Members who will call out God's best in you by reminding you when you forget who God created you to be

   • An atmosphere of growing transparency/tender response to weakness

     ◦ Learn to take off your masks.

     ◦ Learn to share your weaknesses.

     ◦ Practice a tender response to weakness.

---

1 | This was discussed in more detail in Lessons 5–7 of the Heart-to-Heart Community Unit.

- ○ Practice your RARE skills.
- ○ Process life's hurts together.

What do we do in an Identity Group? Each Identity Group will be different, based on the interests, goals, and composition of the group. An Identity Group might be a family, church group, workmates, or community group. Here are some elements that might be practiced when an Identity Group is together:

- Checking in and listening to Jesus as close to daily as possible.
  - ○ Listening to Jesus may mean listening together, or simply sharing what we've sensed from Him recently.
- Check in and listen when you are together as a group.
- Share stories from your week.
  - ○ If I handled it in RARE fashion, here's what I did.
  - ○ I didn't handle it so well; here's what I would like to have done.
- Help each other by listening to Immanuel for His take on the situation.
- Be willing to give each other gentle shame messages.[2]
  - ○ "We are people who behave in this way...."
  - ○ "We don't do...." (the behavior that was hurtful or "not like our people.")
  - ○ "We are your people, and we remind each other of who we are when we forget."
  - ○ No man left behind! We don't leave our people stuck in their sins/iniquities. This would not be adult maturity.
- Read Immanuel Journaling to each other.
- Pray for each other.
- Work on maturity tasks together.

2. **Practice Imitation and Modeling.** It's helpful for us to identify people in our lives who have one or more of the RARE skills and spend time with them. We can ask, "I noticed you really handle anger well...." Or "You don't seem to get discouraged. Tell me how that came about." Ask them to tell stories from their life. Identity Groups are modeling for each other all the time, and our growth will be accelerated when we are intentional about imitation. Remember that Paul said, "Whatever you have learned or received or heard from me, or seen in me—put it into practice." Philippians 4:9a NIV

---

2 | From *The Pandora Problem*, Dr. Jim Wilder

3. The third RARE practice is **Intimacy with Immanuel**, the God who is with us. Together and individually, we can develop the practice of paying attention to what God is whispering to our hearts. This daily intimacy with God helps with everything: helps with our return to joy and peace when life is difficult, helps us process powder keg issues (i.e., triggers) that turn up as we interact more closely with our Identity Group, turns on our relational circuits so that we are open and receptive, and helps us process traumas, where Jesus can give us new perspectives on the painful events of our lives.

Growth in the RARE skills works hand-in-hand with growth in maturity. Together, we are better.

PONDER, JOURNAL, AND DISCUSS:

1. In your life, have you experienced something like an identity group? Over time, your Journey Group may become an identity group, but it is ideal to have some local friends who are "your people" so that your times together are less formal and more extended than Journey Group. Ask Immanuel who might become part of your identity group. Ask Jesus for more opportunities to spend time with these people.

2. As you interact with Jesus, it may help to make a list of people who fit into the following categories:

   ° More ability to remain relational in difficulty than I have

   ° More ability to return to joy from anger, fear, shame, sadness, disgust, or hopeless despair than I have

   ° Has an interactive relationship with Jesus

   ° Ability to gently point out when I'm not being my "best" self

   ° Has suffered without becoming bitter

   As you go through your week, ask the people on your list and others around you to tell you stories of how they have handled hard tasks, suffering, difficult relationships, negative emotions, and growing in Christ. Make notes in your journal when something seems especially important to you.

3. Ask Jesus what He would like you to do to become more intimate with Him. Notice if it seems that He guides you to resting time with Him, Scripture, journaling, nature, exercise, worship, or some other way of deepening your relationship with Him. Slowly put into practice what you sense Him asking of you. It may be a good idea to try one new/different practice at a time so that you can see what increases your sense of His presence and your "mutual mind" with Him. Note your experiences in your journal.

maturity matters
LESSON 4

My Maturity Stories

We pass on our maturity through our example and our stories. It is good to be proactive and intentional about this process. Thinking through your stories is good brain exercise and prepares us for those moments when we want to share how we learned a particular maturity task.

God's plan for transformation is Belonging + Identity. This helps us remember and identify areas in which we want to grow and help others to grow. Remember, when we are at infant or child maturity, we should focus on our own growth. When we reach solid adult maturity, we are better equipped to help others with their journey. It is also helpful to remember that passing through these maturity tasks is what wires our brain.

Important! Even though the maturity stories represent skills that we would have ideally received at certain chronological ages, your maturity stories may come from another time in your life. You will have many Return to Joy stories that occurred at various times of life. Your stories do NOT have to match the chronological time when you first reached that maturity level.

Infant Maturity Stories
- Attachment Stories:
    - Stories of important people in our life with whom we know we have a strong, loving connection
    - Look for a story of both a male and a female in your life
- "Eyes of Heaven" or "Godsight" stories
    - May be the same people from your attachment stories
    - Stories of people who were able to see you as God sees you
- Return to Joy Stories
    - Sadness
    - Fear

- ○ Anger
- ○ Shame
- ○ Disgust
- ○ Despair
- Attunement
  - ○ Times that I felt what someone else was feeling and was with them in it in a comforting way
  - ○ Times I offered validation and comfort

Child Maturity Stories

- Stories of my immediate and extended family
  - ○ Our characteristics and how we came to be that way
  - ○ What it is like us to do in various situations
- My talents and skills
  - ○ Stories of things that seemed to come naturally to me
  - ○ Stories of skills I worked hard to gain
  - ○ Stories of how I used my talents and skills
- Stories of creating belonging for one other person
  - ○ My childhood friends/My siblings
- Stories of asking for what I need/expressing myself
  - ○ Being weak and needing help
  - ○ Expressing my personality (especially when it seemed different from others)
- Stories of controlling my cravings/desires
  - ○ Learning a sport/skill
  - ○ Doing without
- Stories of learning what satisfies
  - ○ What really makes me feel like "me"
  - ○ Satisfaction vs. Pleasure

Adult Maturity Stories

- Stories of my spiritual identity
  - ○ How do I give life?
  - ○ Seeing myself as God sees me

- Stories of My Peer Group/My Tribe/My People
  - How I learned who my people were
  - How we give and receive life/grow together/need each other
  - How we practice "what it is like us to do"
  - How we create belonging for others
- Stories of protecting others from myself
  - When I was upset (angry, scared, sad)
  - Asking for help instead of "pressing through"
- Stories of bringing two or more back to joy
  - Conflict resolution with a win-win solution
  - Attunement, Validation, Comfort in a group
- Stories of suffering well
  - In times of deprivation or difficulty
  - When tough situations don't resolve quickly

Parent Maturity Stories

- Stories of giving without receiving
- Stories of being a calming presence
- Stories of my elders (those who advise me)
- Stories of enjoying/protecting/serving my family
- Stories of helping others mature
  - Providing opportunities for risk and failure with a "safety net"
  - Helping others suffer well and do hard things
  - Seeing others as God sees them
  - Helping others learn their identity/talents/personality
  - Helping others learn to create belonging

Elder Maturity Stories

- Stories of creating belonging for the familyless
  - Through the body of Christ
  - Through your family
- Stories of encouraging my tribe
  - Who we are
  - What it is like us to do

- Stories of "What does Jesus want us to know?"
- Stories from every maturity level

PONDER, JOURNAL, AND DISCUSS:

In this week's Journey Group meeting, you'll be sharing maturity stories. There are 3 options available for how to choose a story to tell:

1. Choose a story to tell from the list above.

2. You can think over the last week or two and think of a time when you handled a situation using adult maturity—using the RARE characteristics.

3. You can think over the last week or two and think of a time when you *didn't* handle a situation in RARE fashion, and tell a story about "What it would be like my True Self to do." In other words, if I had been Acting Like Myself, here's what I would have done. This is a very valuable "replay" or "do-over" type of story that gives your brain (and the listeners' brains) a new model for how to handle the situation. It's also a great way to share your weakness and receive a tender response.

In your story, plan to tell how you felt in your emotions and your body when the situation was happening. It's also good to tell a story that is mild to moderate in intensity—our brains don't train well when they are triggered or overwhelmed.

LESSON 5

Goodbye Fear Bonds, Hello Love!

Have you ever had a vague sense of dread when you knew you were going to interact with a certain person? Do certain people make you feel like you are walking on eggshells? Do you carefully craft your suggestions and conversations with certain people so that they don't take offense? These are just a few of the telltale signs of fear bonds.

Fear bonds occur when our motivation and attachment to a person (and/or theirs to us) is based on the fear of loss, rejection, or other negative responses, rather than because we experience joy and quiet together, we love each other, or we genuinely enjoy each other. The important question to ask in evaluating your relationships is, "What drives my interactions in this relationship?"

Understanding and transforming fears bonds to love bonds is a key component in growing into our true identity—living from the heart Jesus gave us. Identifying all the fear bonds in our lives can be eye-opening and discouraging at the same time, so be prepared to extend grace to yourself and the people in your life as you go through these two lessons.

Exercise — Identifying Fear Bonds

1. Use a notebook for this exercise. Turn to the **Love Bonds** VERSUS **Fear Bonds In Relationships** table at the end of this lesson.

2. Look at the descriptions of Fear Bonds and make notes about your relationships—which relationships have the various Fear Bond characteristics, and any other thoughts that come to mind.

3. Looking honestly at our Fear Bonds is difficult, and you may find yourself feeling shame or hopeless despair. For 5 minutes, do the Relational Circuits exercises and think about some of your favorite appreciation memories.

4. Ask Jesus what these relationships (or you may focus on one relationship) would look like if they were characterized by Love Bonds. Journal the thoughts that come to mind. Also ask Jesus what He would like you to know as you look at the Fear Bonds that may have come to mind.

In our Journey Groups this week, we will talk about the exercise above and think about some first steps to transforming our Fear Bonds to Love Bonds.

Although looking at fear bonds is tough, this is a time of hope, because we can remember that God loves us exactly as we are, He has loved us with all our fear bonds in place, and our value is not based on our maturity, but on the fact that we are created in God's image. Your awareness of God's loving presence will take a leap as your fear bonds slowly dissolve and are replaced with love bonds.

In *Living from the Heart Jesus Gave You*[1] by Dr. James Wilder and others, we learn that maturity is built on our bonds with others. Based on our earliest bonds, we learn to bond two ways; we can bond around the fear of pain, disconnection, or negative emotions, or we can bond around the joy of being together. We can call these types of bonds fear bonds and love or joy bonds.

When we are fear-bonded to others, we find ourselves anxious about the bond, fearful of the emotions arising from the bond, and fearful both of being together and being apart. We worry that negative emotions will weaken or dissolve the bond. When we are together, we are anxious that we will do something to cause a problem, and when we are apart, we fear that the bond isn't strong enough to hold up to separation. We may stay together because we are afraid of being alone, or we could be afraid of what the other person will do if we leave.

When we are joy-bonded, the bond provides a strong foundation of security, even when we are apart. We don't have to fear negative emotions, because we know our bond is safe even in situations that bring negative emotions to the surface. When we are away from each other, we remember each other fondly and know the bond is secure. When we are together, we are able to enjoy each other, be our authentic selves, and share our strengths and weaknesses openly.

Joy bonds are a strong foundation for maturity, so in this lesson, we will look at how to recognize fear bonds, and how to move from fear bonds to joy/love bonds. When one relationship is transformed from fear to joy, we begin to more securely interact in all our relationships, and gradually we move into fearless joy bonds throughout our relationships.

---

1 | *Living from the Heart Jesus Gave You*, Dr. Wilder, et al. This lesson is based entirely on chapter 4.

PONDER, JOURNAL, AND DISCUSS:

1. Do you have any relationships that have secure joy/love bonds? Ask Jesus how He sees the relationships you have that are joy-bonded. Also ask Him how you can grow your joy-bonded relationships to be even more secure. Journal your thoughts.

2. If you have a close relationship that seems more fear-bonded than joy-bonded, ask Jesus how He sees the other person in that relationship. Based on the information in this lesson, what are some steps you can take to begin moving from fear bonds to joy bonds? Journal your thoughts.

LOVE BONDS versus FEAR BONDS IN RELATIONSHIPS[2]

LOVE BONDS	FEAR BONDS
1. Based on love and characterized by truth, closeness, intimacy, joy, peace, perseverance, and authentic giving.	1. Based on fear and characterized by pain, humiliation, desperation, shame, guilt, and/or fear of reaction, abandonment, or other detrimental consequences.
2. Desire driven. (I bond because I want to be with you.)	2. Avoidance driven. (I bond because I want to avoid negative feelings or pain.)
3. Grow stronger both when we move closer and when we move farther away. (When we move closer, I get to know you better. When we move farther away, I am still blessed by the memory of you.)	3. Only grow stronger by moving closer or by moving farther away. (The closer we get, the scarier it gets, so I have to avoid the closeness, or the farther away we get, the scarier it gets, so I have to manipulate closeness.)
4. We can share both positive and negative feelings. The bond is strengthened by this truthful sharing.	4. We cannot share both positive and negative feelings. The bond is strengthened by (1) avoiding negative or positive feelings or (2) by seeking only negative feelings or seeking only positive feelings.

---

2 | *Living from the Heart Jesus Gave You*, p. 68.

5. Participants on both ends of the bond benefit. The bond encourages all to act like themselves.	5. Participants on only one end of the bond gain advantage. The bond actually inhibits people from acting like themselves.
6. Truth pervades the relationship.	6. Deceit and pretending are required.
7. Love Bonds continually grow and mature people, equipping them to find their hearts.	7. Fear Bonds increasingly restrict and stunt growth, keeping people from finding their hearts.
8. Love Bonds operate from the front of the brain (the joy center) and govern "how do I act like myself?"	8. Fear Bonds operate from the back of the brain, and govern "how do I get what I want?"

TYPE A AND TYPE B TRAUMAS[3]

TYPE A TRAUMAS	TYPE B TRAUMAS
Type A trauma is harmful by its *absence*, which causes damage to our emotions. To some degree, one or more of them will typically be found in each stage of our lives, and we can all find at least one Type A trauma wound that needs attention. When you look at the Maturity Indicators Chart, you will see that a failure by the Family and Community—the middle column—produces a Type A trauma. In fact, *absences* in those areas define what Type A traumas are. Here are a few *absences* that illustrate Type A traumas:	Type B trauma is harmful by its *presence*. Having been on the receiving end of the following experiences can create a Type B trauma. There is a range of severity in Type B traumas. It is important to remember that to discount "lesser" traumas is to avoid the truth about how much it hurts, and thereby miss the chance for healing. Avoiding or ignoring wounds does not make them go away. Here are some harmful events that are examples of Type B traumas:
1. Being cherished and celebrated by one's parents simply by virtue of one's existence.	1. Physical abuse, including face slapping, hair pulling, shaking, punching, and tickling a child into hysteria.
2. Having the experience of being a delight.	2. Any spanking which becomes violent, leaving marks or bruises or emotional scars.
3. Having a parent take the time to understand who you are—encouraging you to share who you are, what you think, and what you feel.	3. Sexual abuse including inappropriate touching, sexual kissing or hugging, intercourse, oral or anal sex, voyeurism, exhibitionism, or the sharing of the parent's sexual experiences with a child.

---

3 | *Living from the Heart Jesus Gave You*, Wilder, et al., pp. 85, 88

4. Receiving large amounts of non-sexual, physical nurturing—laps to sit in, arms to hold, and a willingness to let you go when you have had enough.	4. Verbal abuse or name-calling.
5. Being given age-appropriate limits. Having those limits enforced in ways that do not call your value into question.	5. Abandonment by a parent.
6. Being given adequate food, clothing, shelter, medical, and dental care.	6. Torture or satanic ritual abuse.
7. Being taught how to do hard things—to problem solve and to develop persistence.	7. Witnessing someone else being abused.
8. Being taught how to develop personal resources and talents.	

LESSON 6

Looking at Our Relationships

Included with this lesson is a chart entitled "Evaluating My Relationships." At first glance, this chart may look like a terrible thing—who would evaluate their relationships on a chart? However, the chart grew out of several heart characteristics I (Amy) have: I love people and connecting with them as the people God created them to be, I love to see the big picture, I love to make the big picture understandable to others, and I love to understand why things are the way they are. Also, I was a paralegal for many years, and we make charts.

As you look at fear bonds and love/joy bonds, God enables you to begin to understand your personal relationships. This is true of many other relational concepts as well—joy, quieting, attunement, maturity, and attachment/relational styles. You can use this chart to synthesize all these different concepts and take your understanding of relationships to a whole new level, especially when combined with Godsight—seeing people as God sees them. Used wisely, this chart helps you have compassionate curiosity about your relationships—"what are the different components that make this relationship so easy for me, while that other one seems so difficult?"

This week, gently engage with this worksheet. Look at the Evaluating My Relationships chart now. You'll notice that in every column except "We can quiet together," the headings refer to both you and the other person. Using what you've learned in Journey Groups, first make notes about yourself—note your relational style, heart values, and maturity level, and note if the bond seems to be fear-based and whether you build joy with them. Pray for wisdom and God's perspective and begin to complete the chart with regard to the other person.

If your closest relationship is in a place of struggle right now, or you don't have any intimate relationships, ask Jesus to show you patterns in your most "daily" relationships, and ask Him for baby steps of growth toward closeness. Go through the worksheet and ask Him to talk to you about your relationship with Him, if you'd like! Ask Him how a particular relationship might change in these areas as you grow. As you use the worksheet and journaling questions, remember to practice grace and compassion toward yourself and your relationships—we are on a gentle journey toward wholeness. If any of this proves stressful, NOT TO WORRY—put it in a drawer or folder and come back to it in a month or a year. God knows where you are in your relationships, and He will bring this to mind at the right time for you.

There is also a Journaling sheet included as an appendix to help you examine your thoughts and God's thoughts about a specific relationship. You can sit down and journal through all the questions to get a picture of your thoughts and Jesus' thoughts about this relationship. For your closest relationships, you might want to take a week or longer and journal in-depth about each individual question. Some folks may feel ready for that, and others will feel overwhelmed with that idea. Talk with Jesus about your feelings: "Is it a good time for me to go more in-depth with this right now, or would it be better to process what I've learned so far and journal more later?" Remember that Isaiah 30:21 (ESV) tells us, "And your ears shall hear a word behind you, saying, 'This is the way, walk in it,' when you turn to the right or when you turn to the left."

PONDER, JOURNAL, AND DISCUSS:

1. As you've engaged with the chart, have you noticed patterns that extend to several of your relationships? For instance, you might be drawn to people with certain attachment styles or maturity levels. You may notice a family pattern with regard to joy and quiet. Ask Jesus what He wants you to know about any patterns you notice.

2. How might you use the chart and journaling to prepare for a difficult conversation with a friend or family member?

3. How might using the chart and journaling be good preparation for holidays or other times when groups gather? Could this be useful in looking at groups of which you are a part—Bible study, work relationships, friend groups? Ask Immanuel how He might help you to use this in various situations you are facing.

EVALUATING MY RELATIONSHIPS

NAME	INCREASES MY JOY/ I INCREASE THEIRS.	WE CAN QUIET TOGETHER.	FEAR-BASED BOND? ME/THEM	ABILITY TO ATTUNE ME/THEM	ATTACHMENT STYLE ME/THEM	HEART VALUES ME/THEM	MATURITY LEVEL ME/THEM

LESSON 7

Parent & Elder Maturity

In the Infant stage, we learn to receive with joy. At the Child stage, we learn to take care of ourselves. When we are an Adult, we become proficient at taking care of ourselves and one other. When all of these are accomplished, we are ready for the Parent stage of maturity—taking care of another while receiving nothing in return, or as Dr. Jim Wilder said in the webinar Pointing the Way to Maturity: "We are ready to teach a baby to be a human."

When we see the stages of maturity building on one another like this, it's clear that potholes will occur on our life's roadways when we don't accomplish all the tasks in each stage. Learning to receive and ask for what I need as an Infant prepares me to recognize what I need as a Child and meet those needs myself or ask for help. This leads to the ability to recognize those needs in another person, one who can take care of themselves fairly well. This is the mature love of an adult—desiring to meet the needs of another, and allowing them to meet some of our needs. Parent maturity, however, desires to meet the needs of one who can do absolutely nothing to reciprocate.

Below you will find a table which lists the important tasks of Infant, Child, and Adult maturity. As you read through these tasks, ask Immanuel to help you see how important it would be to have these skills in your repertoire as a parent.[1]

INFANT	CHILD	ADULT
Lives in joy. Expands joy capacity.	Asks for what is needed; can say what one feels.	Cares for self and others in a satisfying way.
Develops trust.	Knows what satisfies.	Can return self and others to joy in negative emotions.
Begins to organize self into a person through modeling.	Can do hard things even when doesn't want to.	Develops a group identity; bonds with peers.

1 | From the Maturity Indicators chart, provided in this curriculum, and Maturity Skills Assessment, www.joystartshere.com/site/doc/Maturity%20Skills%20Assessment.pdf

Returns to joy from negative emotions.	Develops personal resources and talents.	Protects others from self.
	Knows self/makes self known.	Contributes to the community.
	Understands the "big picture" of life.	Knows and expresses heart characteristics.

What problems might you expect to see in a family where the parents haven't mastered these tasks well? It's easy to see why each family has its own pattern of "iniquity," which means "bent" or "not growing as it was intended." While this might seem a negative and depressing train of thought, it can actually be very encouraging and hopeful, because gaps can be filled and foundations repaired when the problems are identified. When buying an older home, one has an inspection to see what repairs are going to be needed. This is so much better than moving in, completely unaware of all the structural weaknesses. Now we can see where our family was off track, and gather tools, information, and experts, and begin the hopeful work of repair, so that the structure is stronger than ever before.

A healthy parent has the following maturity tasks to master:

- Protect, serve, and enjoy one's family.

- Devote oneself to taking care of children without expectation that children will reciprocate.

- Allow and provide spiritual parents and siblings for the children—others who are also walking this pathway to wholeness in Christ.

- Learn how to bring children through difficult times and return to joy from other emotions.

It is important to note that many adults who don't have children of their own are at Parent maturity level and are doing the important work of helping children learn tasks their parents haven't successfully mastered. We can be very thankful for all the school teachers, coaches, scout masters, Bible teachers, aunts, uncles, and family friends who step in and meet this critical need. This is God's intention for the community.

When parents successfully bring their children to adult maturity, they may step into the role of Elder to the community. The task of an elder is *sacrificially taking care of the community.* Elders go beyond parent maturity in that they can give sacrificially not only to their own children, but also to others in the community who are in need of a reminder that they are valuable and beloved.

In U.S. culture, elders are often encouraged to abdicate their responsibilities, retire, and enjoy the "good life." What a difference it would make if retirement were viewed as a time to build relationships with those in the community who need models of healthy maturity, Immanuel awareness, and secure attachment.

As adults, we can move more quickly through these maturity tasks because we have the benefit of hindsight and experience to help us identify gaps—we have seen areas where our skills are lacking and our ways aren't bringing joy, peace, and satisfaction into our lives. In addition, unlike children, adults can study the tasks and learn to recognize a more mature person who has a missing skill.

PONDER, JOURNAL, AND DISCUSS:

As we finish up this unit on Maturity Matters, what is your plan for future maturity growth? Here are some questions to help you form a plan:

1. What is the highest level of maturity I could have based on my age and my family structure?

2. What is my current maturity level? An example might be, "I'm at adult maturity with a child maturity gap in doing hard things and an infant maturity gap in handling fear."

3. What maturity tasks do I want to work on next? Some things to consider: You can work on more than one task at once. This can be done by balancing your plan between four types of tasks: (1) those where you don't know what the task looks like in daily life and (2) those where you have a good "picture" in mind, but just need practice, (3) "major" foundational tasks like learning to handle negative emotions, and (4) the more easily accomplished tasks like contributing to the community.

4. What are some practical baby steps I can take in working on these maturity tasks?

God's heart & my heart
UNIT FIVE

God's heart & my heart
LESSON 1

God's Heart: Everlasting Sticky Love

In this unit, we will look at God's heart and our hearts; we'll consider the characteristics of our hearts both when we are cooperating with the Holy Spirit and when we are living life independently of His Spirit.

God's heart is incredibly *consistent* toward us; it is described by the Hebrew word *hesed* (pronounced "hessid"). The website hesed.com defines *hesed* as "the consistent, ever-faithful, relentless, constantly-pursuing, lavish, extravagant, unrestrained, furious love of our Father God."[1]

In her book, *Walking in the Dust of the Rabbi Jesus*, author Lois Tverberg says that *hesed* "acts out of unswerving loyalty even to the most undeserving...."[2] As Romans 5:8 NIV says, "But God demonstrates his own love for us in this: While we were still sinners, Christ died for us."

Dr. Jim Wilder says in *The Pandora Problem* that "Attachment love *endures*, so *hesed* is often translated "enduring love." Yet, for attachment to be good love, it must not simply endure but also be deeply kind. Thus hesed is also translated as "loving kindness."[3]

Messianic Rabbi Gene Binder of Cornerstone Boulder says that "Love can't be fully actuated until it has something to express itself on [or toward]."[4] Rabbi Binder also makes an interesting connection—God is *expansive* love, and scientists have stated that the universe is constantly expanding. What if God's *hesed* love expands the boundaries of love? He uses the example of the Sermon on the Mount, where we see the common guidelines for how to treat our neighbor greatly expanded.

---

1 | www.hesed.com/hesed/

2 | *Walking in the Dust of Rabbi Jesus,* Zondervan, 2012

3 | *The Pandora Problem*, p. 21.

4 | Sermon, 10/20/15 – tinyurl.com/4c6mgtqc

Matthew 5:38-48 ESV states:

> [38]"You have heard that it was said, 'An eye for an eye and a tooth for a tooth.' [39]But I say to you, Do not resist the one who is evil. But if anyone slaps you on the right cheek, turn to him the other also. [40]And if anyone would sue you and take your tunic, let him have your cloak as well. [41]And if anyone forces you to go one mile, go with him two miles. [42]Give to the one who begs from you, and do not refuse the one who would borrow from you.
>
> [43]"You have heard that it was said, 'You shall love your neighbor and hate your enemy.' [44]But I say to you, Love your enemies and pray for those who persecute you, [45]so that you may be sons of your Father who is in heaven. For he makes his sun rise on the evil and on the good, and sends rain on the just and on the unjust. [46]For if you love those who love you, what reward do you have? Do not even the tax collectors do the same? [47]And if you greet only your brothers, what more are you doing than others? Do not even the Gentiles do the same? [48]You therefore must be perfect, as your heavenly Father is perfect."[5]

We receive *hesed* love from God, and it fills us up to overflowing so that we can be fully mature, or perfect, and share this expanded *hesed* love with others. Dr. Wilder says, "The main effect of Christian life is (or should be) growing love in people who are less loving, less joyful, and less protective than people should be."[6]

As we examine God's *hesed* love, we discover another surprising, challenging fact: "Hesed is loyalty built around weakness."[7] Throughout the Old Testament, we see God's love reaching out for the weak nation of Israel, raising up Joseph to provide for them in Egypt, and later Moses to bring them out of Egypt. Even when Israel insisted on being like the larger, more powerful nations in desiring a king, God's loyal love endured and brought them out of bondage. In *The Pandora Problem*, Dr. Wilder says we can be like God: "Discovery of a weakness in a hesed group brings help. Weakness creates places to help each other grow. Sharing weaknesses builds joyful, sheltering bonds. Loyalty grows out of joy to be together."[8]

In reviewing all these characteristics of hesed love, do you feel a bit intimidated? Perhaps overwhelmed? A love that is consistent, kind, enduring,

---

5 | Bible Gateway tells us that this word perfect can also be translated as "whole, complete, fully mature, lacking nothing, all-inclusive, well rounded."

6 | *The Pandora Problem*, p. 17.

7 | Ibid.

8 | Ibid.

expansive, and unswervingly loyal to the undeserving? This seemed unattainable to me, until my attention was drawn to one statement from *The Pandora Problem*:

"Weakness creates places to help each other grow."[9]

The first thing we need in our quest to develop hesed love is a group with weaknesses. If that is our prerequisite, perhaps we can do this after all! As we learn to receive God's hesed love for us and accept that it is unswervingly loyal even when we are undeserving, we will find ourselves able to let go of the need to be best or right, to perform, and importantly, the need to hide our weaknesses. If my weakness does not endanger God's hesed love for me, then your weakness need not endanger my hesed love for you.

As we are filled with His absolute acceptance of us, we will grow in our capacity to remain loving to others, and even to build loyalty around weakness. What does it mean to build loyalty around weakness? When one person in a group allows others to see their weakness and the group responds tenderly, something happens in the group. It reminds the members of God's love and that we aren't defined by our weaknesses. This changes the entire group dynamic. Predator and possum tendencies are gradually overcome by protector skills, and the group has loyalty around weakness, loyalty that says, "Your weakness does not disqualify you here, we will protect you as you grow into the person God created you to be. We will remind you of your truest self."

Growth in protector skills begins with building our capacity to stay connected relationally in difficult situations. As a reminder, we grow joy capacity by practicing the following four key elements individually and with our group:

- Notice and build your ability to keep *relational circuits on*.
- Practice *appreciation* throughout the day.
- Increase your capacity to *quiet* during difficult circumstances.
- Look for opportunities to build *joy* as often as possible.

It is encouraging to remember that we share God's limitless capacity as we grow in these elements and turn our faces toward Him and receive His never-ending hesed love.

PONDER, JOURNAL, AND DISCUSS:

1. Meditate on this definition of God's hesed love: "the consistent, ever-faithful, relentless, constantly-pursuing, lavish, extravagant, unrestrained, furious love of our Father God." Ask God what He would like you to know about His love.

---

9 | Ibid.

2. Have you had an experience where someone was protective around your weakness, whether physical, mental, or emotional? What does it feel like to be protected in your weak areas? Ask Jesus how you can grow in your protection of others' weaknesses.

God's heart & my heart
LESSON 2

Living Life From God's Perspective

Chris Coursey writes, "Hope and direction come from seeing situations, ourselves and others the way they were meant to be instead of only seeing what went wrong."[1] Our own perspective is limited and skewed by our past experiences and wounds, our plans, our culture, and even our current mood. God generously shares His perspective with us as we develop the practice of tuning in to Him.

Living life from God's perspective (also called Godsight) doesn't mean we view life through rose-tinted glasses and refuse to acknowledge the pain of life, but that we see there is more happening than the current circumstances reveal. I think of how Joseph maintained his integrity in Potiphar's household and in prison, trusting that God was at work even when all evidence seemed to indicate that Joseph had been forgotten.

God is not hiding His thoughts from us, and His Word reminds us of this:

John 10:27 – "My sheep hear my voice, and I know them, and they follow me."

Jeremiah 33:3 – "Call to me and I will answer you, and will tell you great and hidden things that you have not known."

However, Job 33:14 reminds us that "God speaks in one way, and in two, though man does not perceive it." The problem is not in God's willingness to share what He is thinking, but in our ability to perceive His voice and/or to receive and accept His thoughts.

Perceiving His Voice[2]

Dr. Jim Wilder has likened the human brain to a cell phone; when a cell phone is in Airplane Mode, messages are still being sent to it, and it still

---

1 | *Transforming Fellowship*, p. 172.

2 | A review of Unit 3, Lesson 5: Listening to the Shepherd will provide helpful guidance in recognizing God's voice.

has the technology to receive messages, but those functions are turned off.[3] When our relational circuits are dimmed or off, we are like a phone in Airplane Mode, and it's unlikely we will perceive even God's clearest messages, so restoration of relational mode/relational circuits is our first task. This can usually be achieved by using Shalom My Body or stretching and deep breathing exercises, and spending some time meditating on and "fully entering" appreciation memories or memories of connection with God. "Fully entering" means that we bring up a memory and think of what we saw, heard, smelled, tasted, touched, and felt emotionally during the experience, remembering every aspect we can bring to mind. Sitting in an appreciation memory for at least three minutes is a practice that will help our brains become moldable, teachable, and more able to tune in to God's thoughts. It's tempting to jump quickly from appreciation to trying to sense God, but spending those three minutes warming up our brain is time well spent.

Over time, each of us is likely to find that certain practices help us tune in and perceive God's voice. Some people "hear" most clearly when they write or type in a journal. Other activities that have been associated with listening to God are taking a walk, lying down, listening to music, sitting in silence, baking, or cleaning house; each person should experiment and find what seems to help them tune in. Ed Khouri returns us to cellphone analogies by referring to "5-bar moments"—we go wherever the reception is best![4]

When we sense we have made a connection with God, we take note of whatever thoughts seem to come into our mind. It is helpful to practice this process with a friend or two, and share every thought that arises, whether or not we understand if or how they would fit. Remember Isaiah 55:8-9 ESV:

> For my thoughts are not your thoughts,
>   neither are your ways my ways, declares the Lord.
> For as the heavens are higher than the earth,
>   so are my ways higher than your ways
>   and my thoughts than your thoughts.

This verse isn't saying that we can never access God's thoughts, but that we might not recognize them, especially if we have been taught that God speaks in only a few certain ways. Through the years, God's people have heard the "still, small voice" of 1 Kings 19, seen visions, writing on the wall, talking donkeys, had dreams, felt Scripture speak, and received thoughts from God through other believers.

In the book *Joyful Journey*, hearing God's voice is explained using neuroscience:

---

3 | You can listen to this teaching at www.youtube.com/watch?v=6hig_etuTUc

4 | "Restarting" module of the Connexus video curriculum, available from www.humbleshack.net

"The structure in the brain called the cingulate cortex makes it possible for meaningful communication to occur between two different minds by establishing a mutual-mind state. When establishing a mutual-mind state, we learn to think and feel the way people we love think and feel. The interesting aspect of the mutual-mind state in the brain is that it works faster than the conscious mind so that we are never sure whether a mutual-mind thought is theirs or ours."[5]

When discussing the idea of hearing God's voice, have you ever said, "But I don't know if it is my thought or God's thought?" Surprise! That's just what it is like to have mutual-mind with another person or with God—we know one another well enough to *think their thoughts with them.*

We can know God well enough to experience a mutual-mind state with Him, which is a beautiful concept. However, if I have mutual-mind with a friend, I don't have the right to speak for my friend, and I have an obligation to check with my friend to verify that what I'm sensing is actually what she is thinking. How does this translate into verifying God's thoughts? Here are some guidelines for evaluating thoughts that you sense are from God:

- **Community, community, community!** Sharing what you hear from God with friends over a period of time and inviting them to share their thoughts is a powerful way to receive validation or caution. Be authentic, vulnerable, and open to input as you share with your group.

- **Congruency with Scripture.** If the thoughts you sensed from God line up with God's overall character in the Word, it is likely you are sharing mutual-mind with Him. Notice how I've worded this sentence, however; it lines up with *God's overall character*—we can't cherry-pick a verse to line up with what we've heard, and we hold our God-thoughts loosely—it is *likely* you are sharing mutual-mind, but not time to put up a billboard that says, "Thus saith the Lord"!

- **Gentleness and humility.** These characteristics of God are so important to this topic that I'm giving them special attention. When we are in a mutual-mind state with Him, we will find ourselves expressing our thoughts in a gentle, humble way. Where there is strife and pressure to force others to accept our position, God's character is not in the forefront. This is a good time to return to Him and ask, "Am I off track? What do you want me to know?"

- **The Shalom Test.** Even if God is challenging us or bringing conviction, His thoughts tend to bring peace. This is another area where community is so helpful—our own history, traumas, and

---

5 | *Joyful Journey,* Dr. Jim Wilder, Sungshim and John Loppnow, Anna Kang, p. 3.

iniquities can affect how we receive God's thoughts, so it is wise to ask trusted friends if the mutual-mind thoughts you are sensing from God seem to pass the Shalom Test for them.

As we consistently seek mutual-mind with God, we will begin more easily to see life from His perspective, to sense His guidance, and to welcome His thoughts about the situations and people that are bringing disquiet to our souls. As we experience the goodness and kindness of His thoughts, our trust in Him will grow, and our character will become more like His everlasting, steadfast love.

PONDER, JOURNAL, AND DISCUSS:

1. Have you had times when you recognized that you were tuned in to God's thoughts, in a mutual-mind state with Him? What was that like? If you haven't experienced this state, have you known others who expressed God's thoughts to you in a way that it truly seemed like they were hearing from Him? What feeling words would you associate with this experience?

2. Review this lesson again with God, asking Him to highlight any thoughts He'd like you to consider more carefully. (If you are feeling negatively stirred up, go to an appreciation memory first.) Ask Him what He wants you to know, if there's any action He wants you to take, or if He just wants to sit with you as you meditate. Note the thoughts that come to mind.

3. What people come to mind who might practice listening for God's thoughts with you? If none come to mind, are there people in your Journey Group who might want to meet outside the group by Zoom and give this a try? Ask Immanuel to bring to mind those people who would be good partners for you.

God's heart & my heart
LESSON 3

The Sark: Common Configurations & Sark in Scripture

The word "sark" is taken from the Greek, and is translated "flesh" in the New Testament. Because of this translation, "sark" is largely understood to be sins we commit with our "flesh" or body—sexual sin, drunkenness, gluttony, etc. These sins are one aspect of the word "flesh," but another, more elusive aspect is defined in *Vine's Complete Expository Dictionary* as "the *weaker element in human nature*" and "*the lower and temporary element in the Christian*," and "*the outward and seeming*," as opposed to the inward and real. These definitions are the elements of the sark that oppose Godsight—His eternal perspective of mankind, our lives, and the world. "Stop the Sark" may be the most difficult relational skill to understand because it is "running in the background" of our mind.

In Chris Coursey's book *Transforming Fellowship*,[1] he notes:

> "Just as Skill 13 is seeing what God sees that guides us to a peaceful destination, Skill 14 is the skill that turns us around when we are lost. Sometimes we think we are heading in the right direction when in fact we are going the wrong way. This Greek word sark ... refers to seeing life according to our view of *who people are* and *how things should be*."

Chris further notes that just as the Pharisees of Jesus' time firmly believed they knew right from wrong, so our sark can lead us to believe that we *know* the right thing in a given situation, when in fact we may be far from Godsight. Extreme examples might be the murder of physicians who perform abortions and other acts of terrorism that spring from religious fanaticism, but we certainly don't have to be fanatics to fall victim to our sark.

When Jesus was asked about the greatest commandment, He responded that love for God and love for other people were the essence of all the commandments. When we find ourselves more concerned about who or what is *right* rather than how to walk in *love*, we can be assured that our sark is in play.

---

1 | *Transforming Fellowship*, p. 181

The sark operates from the accumulation of our experiences in life rather than what God knows to be true. For instance, we may mistrust people of a certain gender, race, or religion because of our personal history, or we may think God is harsh and disappointed because of our experiences. Because the sark sees others as the sum of their past actions, sark thinking is characterized by criticism, judgment, gossip, resentment, legalism, self-justification, and self-righteousness.[2]

Because of this focus on our own experience and history, there are as many configurations of the sark as there are human beings. However, there are some common manifestations we may recognize:

- The *biblically informed sark* is dangerous because the more Scripture we know *without intimacy with Immanuel* which brings Godsight, the more likely we are to be certain we know right from wrong. The biblically informed sark is often certain that its opinions are morally right, pleasing to God, and should be enforced on others. Keeping the relationship intact is often considered to be of secondary importance.[3] Without love, the biblically informed sark will lead to predatory behavior.

- The *undirected sark* creates problems because without direction, guidelines and goals, our sark will seek the path of least resistance in order to avoid pain. This may mean that truth loses out, because the truth is often hard and leads to difficult choices. Undirected, the sark may also leave relationships too quickly or refuse to set boundaries. The undirected sark may lead to codependency, possum behavior, and elastic moral standards.

- The *dependent sark* is one result of what I call the *poorly loved heart*. The dependent sark believes that it will never know what is right, and therefore gives over decision making to others. This may lead to abdicating responsibility, having a victim mentality (or actually being a victim of abuse), and other possum behaviors.

- The *independent sark* is a *poorly loved heart* which has made vows such as, "I have to figure life out for myself," "No one else will tell me what to do," or "I can make better decisions than anyone else." The independent sark tends to be very prickly and proud and is likely to exhibit predatory behavior.

Learning to stop the sark is done in community—we watch humble people who continually look for Immanuel's presence and input, and quickly acknowledge when they act from the sark. We also learn to stop the sark when mature, loving members of our community can gently bring our own sark tendencies to our attention.

---

2 | *Transforming Fellowship*, p. 182

3 | Ibid.

In *Transforming Fellowship,* Chris says,

> "We rely on people who have the skill to guide us. With trusted friends and family members, we turn to these lampposts for 'a witness' in our decisions and relationships. There is wisdom for [this skill] in the passage where Jesus says, 'Again, I tell you that if two of you on earth agree about anything you ask for, it will be done for you by my Father in Heaven. For where two or three come together in my name, there am I with them.' (Matthew 18:19-20, NIV). This is not simply a verse about finding people to agree with us so we get what we want; it is an example of mutual mind between people and the Living God where we are 'on the same page.'"[4]

SARK IN SCRIPTURE

We know that Scripture is the inspired word of God. As we study the Bible, we must be careful to remember that while many portions tell us God's thoughts, some other verses illustrate a discussion between God and man, or man's thoughts without Godsight. For instance, a number of the Psalms begin with the cries of David or others who feel abandoned or punished by God. Look at Psalm 88 ESV:

> "O LORD, God of my salvation;
>   I cry out day and night before you.
> Let my prayer come before you;
>   incline your ear to my cry! ...
> You have caused my companions to shun me;
>   you have made me a horror to them ...
> O LORD, why do you cast my soul away?
>   Why do you hide your face from me? ...
> Your wrath has swept over me;
>   your dreadful assaults destroy me.
> They surround me like a flood all day long;
>   they close in on me together.
> You have caused my beloved and my friend to shun me;
>   my companions have become darkness."

Does this Psalm carry the voice of a person who is experiencing Godsight? No, this is a sark attack, and the psalmist feels as though all his current difficulties are being visited upon him by God, and that God has turned away from him.

Other psalms reveal a process of return to joy and connection with our God who is with us. If we read only a portion of such psalms, we might find ourselves hearing the sark of the psalmist, rather than his thoughts after receiving Godsight. For instance, Psalm 13 ESV says:

---

4 | *Transforming Fellowship,* p. 187.

> "How long, O Lord? Will you forget me forever?
>   How long will you hide your face from me?
> How long must I take counsel in my soul
>   and have sorrow in my heart all the day?
> How long shall my enemy be exalted over me?

STUCK IN PAIN

> Consider and answer me, O Lord my God;
>   light up my eyes, lest I sleep the sleep of death,
> lest my enemy say, 'I have prevailed over him,'
>   lest my foes rejoice because I am shaken.

REACHING OUT TO GOD

> But I have trusted in your steadfast love;
>   my heart shall rejoice in your salvation.
> I will sing to the Lord,
>   because he has dealt bountifully with me."

RETURN TO JOY AND GODSIGHT

Perhaps you have heard it taught, "You know the Word says that God can't look on sin." This teaching comes from the book of Habakkuk, which begins with Habakkuk making complaints against God, and each complaint is answered by the Lord. Notice Habakkuk 1:2-4 (NIV), where Habakkuk looks at what is happening in the world around him, and he is certain that God's will and His justice are no longer at work.

> How long, Lord, must I call for help, but you do not listen?
> Or cry out to you, "Violence!" but you do not save?
> Why do you make me look at injustice?
> **Why do you tolerate wrongdoing?**
> Destruction and violence are before me;
> there is strife, and conflict abounds.
> Therefore **the law is paralyzed,**
> and **justice never prevails.**
> The wicked hem in the righteous,
> so that justice is perverted.

God's response is rather surprising (1:5):

> "Look at the nations and watch—and be utterly amazed. For I am going to do something in your days that you would not believe, even if you were told."

Interestingly, Habakkuk indeed does not believe God! He continues his complaint in verse 1:13:

> "You who are of purer eyes than to see evil and cannot look at wrong, why do you idly look at traitors and remain silent when the wicked swallows up the man more righteous than he?"

Habakkuk's sark is telling him that *surely* God would never allow the wicked to win over the righteous, that he knows right from wrong, and this situation is clearly *wrong*. This is sure evidence of the sark at work: "I can determine right from wrong without God's input, perhaps even in spite of God's input!" Ever since the Fall, the sark has chosen to eat from the Tree of the Knowledge of Good and Evil, rather than choosing to trust in God's goodness. Being aware of the sark and asking Jesus for His perspective is the first step to stopping the sark.

PONDER, JOURNAL, AND DISCUSS:

1. Which of the common configurations of the sark have you noticed in yourself?

   ° Biblically informed sark

   ° Undirected sark

   ° Dependent sark

   ° Independent sark

2. After reading the portion from *Transforming Fellowship* below, what are some ways this might be put into practice in your life?

   "We rely on people who have the skill to guide us. With trusted friends and family members, we turn to these lampposts for 'a witness' in our decisions and relationships. There is wisdom for [this skill] in the passage where Jesus says, 'Again, I tell you that if two of you on earth agree about anything you ask for, it will be done for you by my Father in Heaven. For where two or three come together in my name, there am I with them.' (Matthew 18:19-20, NIV). This is not simply a verse about finding people to agree with us so we get what we want; it is an example of mutual mind between people and the Living God where we are 'on the same page.'" (*TF*, p. 187)

God's heart & my heart
LESSON 4

Value vs. Wholeness vs. Identity

Living from the Heart Jesus Gave You tells us that we need to know who we are, we need to be reminded when we forget, and we need repair for our broken hearts. "That is what it takes to achieve wholeness in a fractured world. It takes belonging to a community. It takes a whole lot of work in the area of maturity. It takes God's hand to boost people when they are stuck, and it takes a lifetime."[1]

Value vs. Identity vs. Wholeness

The concepts of our value, our identity, and living in wholeness can become tangled up in our minds and cause us to sink into despair when life's storms are blowing. When we feel like we've let ourselves, others, and God down, we can slide into this confusing tangle—has our value or identity changed? Will we ever walk in wholeness? Let's look at these concepts.

OUR **VALUE**:

Our VALUE is inherent, unchanging, everlasting, and complete. It is also unrelated to our salvation—every person is inherently, totally, unchangingly, and everlastingly valuable.

OUR **IDENTITY**:

Each of us has an identity that is unique to us and like our DNA, all the possibilities unique to our identity exist within us at birth, but not all will be manifested. When a baby is born, his DNA is uniquely his own, but not every possibility inherent in that DNA will manifest over the course of his life. The manifestation of gifting, talent, ability, intelligence, and physical and mental health or illness will be strongly affected by how he is parented, the health and wealth of his community, school, culture and country, the time in histo-

---

1 | *Living from the Heart Jesus Gave You*, p. 5.

ry into which he is born, and many other variables. Our individual identity is like a hidden treasure that may or may not be discovered, developed, and delighted in; it is a treasure even if it remains hidden.

While each person has their own unique identity, all believers share the same identity in Christ, and every one of us can find our identity in Christ from the Word of God. However, just as is true in our unique identity, our identity in Christ may not be fully manifested during our lifetime. Now the concept of wholeness enters our picture.

OUR **WHOLENESS:**

Wholeness begins to reveal itself as we trust in our value, as we manifest our unique identity and our identity in Christ. Wholeness is the ability to externally exhibit our value and identity, but wholeness doesn't determine our value or identity.

We are each on a spectrum of wholeness, and no two people enter life at the same spot on that spectrum. Depending on the health and wholeness of our family and community, we may walk in age-appropriate wholeness for most of our life, or we may never experience the tiniest glimpse of wholeness. However, let us cling to the truth that our *value* (and the value of those around us) is inherent, unchanging, everlasting, and complete.

Perhaps this is some of what Paul was addressing when he said, "And we urge you, brothers, admonish the idle, encourage the fainthearted, help the weak, be patient with them all. See that no one repays anyone evil for evil, but always seek to do good to one another and to everyone." (1 Thessalonians 5:14-15 ESV) Some of us need admonishment, some need encouragement, some assistance, but all of us need patience.

As *Living from the Heart Jesus Gave You* says, this work takes a lifetime. It's important for all of us to remember that we were each born into families with certain gifts and limitations, and the events that occur in our lifetimes affect our growth. Some of us are born with a head start—we might have a family that is warmly loving and deeply connected with God, while others are born far behind the starting line—our family might be highly dysfunctional, with no idea that our value and identity come from God. Looking at each other from the outside, we might be tempted to judge one another, but only God knows our starting line in life, and what detours have occurred in our race. It is not how far we make it in this marathon that counts, but the attitude of our heart and how we seek to fully rely on God for our value, our identity, and our growth in wholeness.

PONDER, JOURNAL, AND DISCUSS:

> Therefore, since we are surrounded by such a great cloud of witnesses, let us throw off everything that hinders and the sin that so easily entangles. And *let us run with perseverance the race marked out for us, fixing our eyes on Jesus, the pioneer and perfecter of faith.* For the joy set before him he endured the cross, scorning its shame, and sat down at the right hand of the throne of God. Consider him who endured such opposition from sinners, so that you will not grow weary and lose heart.

Hebrews 12:1-3 NIV *emphasis added*

1. Read the above Scripture passage.

2. Go to an appreciation memory, a time where you felt joyful, peaceful, connected and/or accepted. Sit with this memory for 3 minutes, allowing yourself to fully enter into it with all your senses.

3. From this appreciation memory, ask God these questions:

   ○ Jesus, what do you want me to know about my value? Are there lies I've believed about my value? What is the truth?

   ○ Father, what is the race you have marked out for *me*? What do you want me to know about my identity and this race? Jesus, how can you help me fix my eyes on You while I'm in this race?

   ○ Father, Son, and Holy Spirit, what do you want to bring to my mind about my wholeness? Is there an area in my life where I can cooperate with You to bring more wholeness?

4. Return to the appreciation memory and fully enter in. Sit there quietly for 3 minutes, noticing if any further thoughts come to mind.

LESSON 5

Wholeness vs. Identity: My True Identity

A person who is living from their whole heart is truly a beautiful sight—a gift of light to their family and community. Lesson 4 looked at aspects of wholeness such as maturity, healing from trauma, and belonging. We will continue to grow into wholeness for our entire lives as we continue to deepen our relationship with Immanuel and with those around us.

What is true identity? True identity is what emerges when we live from our heart, "when the spiritual eyes of our hearts are turned toward God, we see truth and receive guidance and discernment ... joy motivates our hearts to watch God endlessly. Watching God springs from a love-bond with God. Jesus highlighted this truth when He said that wherever our treasure was, there we would find our hearts also (Luke 12:34) ... Only with our hearts turned to God can we have confidence in what we know. We can see what is good, what we should do, and who we are."[1]

This beautiful quote from *Living from the Heart Jesus Gave You* helps us see how wholeness and true identity or "true knowing" are intertwined. Taking steps toward wholeness helps clean up our image of God from all the tarnish brought by the pain of trauma, lies of the sark, fearful attachment styles, and lack of maturity. Our true identity is revealed and more fully manifested in our daily lives as we are able to fully embrace the reality that Immanuel is glad to be with us regardless of our behavior, our performance as a believer, or our position on the journey to wholeness.

In *Living from the Heart Jesus Gave You*, the conditions that lead to *true knowing* are these:

1. Our hearts must be the healthy hearts that Jesus gave us.

2. Our hearts must be turned toward God with all our love and strength.

3. We must weed out and avoid the words and judgments of the sark.[2]

---

1 | *Living from the Heart Jesus Gave You*, pp. 129-130

2 | Ibid., p. 131

Some of us will look at these conditions and become fearful that our performance of them is not adequate, but nothing could be further from the truth. Remember that we are on a continuum of *true knowing*—it is not a point out in front of us that we must reach on our own, but a gradual revealing of what is already within us through God's tremendous grace. Let's look at these conditions again:

1. Our hearts must be the healthy hearts that Jesus gave us. *We receive our new healthy heart as a free gift from God at the point of salvation.*

2. Our hearts must be turned toward God with all our love and strength. *As we receive healing and travel toward wholeness, our hearts will turn toward God with ever more love and strength. Don't you feel within yourself that desire to love God with every ounce of your strength? There is no condemnation here for "less than perfect" love for God.*

3. We must weed out and avoid the words and judgments of the sark. Again, as we receive wholeness, we begin to recognize the sark and its constant efforts to understand life and make judgments without Immanuel's input. And again, no condemnation as we weed out the sark from our mind—as stated in Romans 7 below, in our inner being, we delight in God and His ways.

Read through Romans 7:20-8:2 below (ESV, emphasis added):

Now if I do what I do not want, it is no longer I who do it, but sin that dwells within me. So I find it to be a law that when I want to do right, evil lies close at hand. For *I delight in the law of God, in my inner being,* but I see in my members another law waging war against the law of my mind and making me captive to the law of sin that dwells in my members. Wretched man that I am! Who will deliver me from this body of death? *Thanks be to God through Jesus Christ our Lord!* So then, I myself serve the law of God with my mind, but with my flesh I serve the law of sin. There is therefore now no condemnation for those who are in Christ Jesus. For the law of the Spirit of life has set you free in Christ Jesus from the law of sin and death.

We have both *been set free* and are *being set free!* As we learn to trust God and rely on what He reveals to us, we will walk in the freedom of the Spirit. This freedom is described in Proverbs 3:5-6:

"Trust in the LORD with all your *heart* and lean not on your *own understanding* [sark]; in all your ways *acknowledge (discern, know, focus your heart on]* Him and He will direct your paths." (Prov. 3:5-6, emphasis from *Living from the Heart Jesus Gave You*, p. 132)

The contrast between the healthy heart and the sark can also be seen in Isaiah 30:15-16 (ESV, brackets added):

> For thus said the Lord GOD, the Holy One of Israel,
> "In returning and rest you shall be saved;
> > in quietness and in trust shall be your strength." [Healthy Heart]
>
> But you were unwilling, and you said,
> "No! We will flee upon horses"; [Sark]
> > therefore you shall flee away;
>
> and, "We will ride upon swift steeds"; [Sark]
> > therefore your pursuers shall be swift.

Here in Isaiah, we see that the Lord tells the people of Israel how to live from their true, healthy hearts—to return, rest, quiet themselves, and trust in Him. Contrasted with this is the sark—reliance on their own strength, fighting in their own power. God offers us each a life of trust and rest, and He will also allow us to wear ourselves out seeking our own strength and ways. Let us listen to Him and grow into our true identity!

PONDER, JOURNAL, AND DISCUSS:

1. Has there been a time in your life when you felt like you were in some alignment with your true identity? If so, what were some characteristics of that time in your life?

2. What activities seem to make you feel more "yourself"? This might mean these activities make you feel alive, energized, and passionate, or they might make you feel peaceful and at rest.

3. Our joy capacity must grow in order for our joy to "motivate our hearts to watch God endlessly." (*Living from the Heart Jesus Gave You*). What activities bring you a sense of "glad to be together" joy? What are some ways you can insert more joy-building activities into your daily life?

God's heart & my heart
LESSON 6

Understanding Heart Characteristics, Part 1

As we look at our true identity, it is helpful to remember that as new creations, our identity in Christ is secure. I encourage you to revisit the "Who I Am in Christ" list from Unit 3, Lesson 4.[1] Each of the truths on this list is *always* true of *every single one* of us. It is helpful to interact with Immanuel about our identity in Christ, so I encourage you to take this list and ask God what He wants you to know about these truths. You might want to journal with Him about each truth individually. This is a task which can take many months, not one that you try to accomplish quickly.

In addition to our identity in Christ as believers, there are also characteristics we each receive from God which vary from person to person. There are infinite facets of God's personality and character, and He delights to implant in each person a very specific combination of His character and personality. As I asked Immanuel what He wanted me to know about these heart characteristics that are in each of us in wide variety, I sensed the following:

> "My daughter, you all belong to each another. You are all an intricate body, and each one carries traits of Me that will manifest My presence in your particular corner of the world, and will bring joy, peace, belonging and healing to people with whom you interact. As you seek and develop these heart characteristics, you become more of the person I created you to be, you connect more strongly with Me, and you impact your community in the ways I chose for you. It is a delight to Me to see each of you looking for the treasures hidden within yourselves and each other. Enjoy this treasure hunt together!"

In the 4-level control center of the brain, our heart characteristics are developed in Level 4, otherwise known as the Identity Center. This is the

---

1 | "Who I am in Christ," Neil Anderson, www.ficm.org

part of our brain that knows "what it is like me and my people to do," so a well-trained Level 4 is tuned in to the special traits God has placed within us. As we learn to use these traits in our interactions, we partner with God to create belonging and restore shalom—the sense that things are as they should be. What a tremendous gift to our fractured world!

In her video curriculum *Attune to Attach*,[2] Maribeth Poole teaches about our Identity Center and our heart characteristics. Along with this lesson you'll find Maribeth's list of heart characteristics and concepts that may help you begin to identify what God has planted in your heart.

As you look at this list, consider these questions:

1. Which of these words or traits resonate with you?

2. Are there concepts here that feel especially important to you?

3. What breaks your heart? Would it really upset you if you could not *be* one of these words? For example, one person might feel very sad to lose *tradition*, while another might be heartbroken at the idea of a world without *uniqueness*.

4. Is there a concept here that you would be willing to fight for, whether for yourself or for others? For instance, God placed a strong desire for *justice* in some of us, while others might see *mercy* as more important.

5. Do you see a word here that you absolutely love when people apply it to you? My daughter Olivia has many heart characteristics, but she feels particularly satisfied when people notice and enjoy her sense of humor!

Spend some time this week journaling with God about these questions. Ask Him to help you notice your heart characteristics as they manifest in your daily life. Also ask Him to bring to mind those things that hurt you, that break your heart. What does He want you to know about the particular combination of His personality traits that He has placed within you? Where might these traits be particularly helpful as you interact with others?

This week in Journey Group, we will discuss what you have sensed from God as you interacted with Him about your heart characteristics.

---

2 | *Attune to Attach* DVD course, www.maribethpoole.com

Heart Characteristics

Achievement	Future generations	Personal fulfillment
Adaptability	Generosity	Power
Adventure	Giving back	Presence
Altruism	Grace	Pride
Ambition	Gratefulness	Recognition
Authenticity	Gratitude	Reliability
Availability	Growth	Resilience
Balance	Harmony	Resourcefulness
Beauty	Health	Respect
Being the best	Home	Respectability
Belonging	Honesty	Rest
Career	Hope	Risk taking
Caring	Hospitality	Safety
Collaboration	Humility	Security
Comfort	Humor	Self-awareness
Commitment	Inclusion	Self-discipline
Community	Independence	Self-expression
Compassion	Initiative	Self-limitation
Competence	Integrity	Self-respect
Confidence	Intimacy	Sensitivity
Connection	Intuition	Serenity
Contentment	Job security	Service
Contribution	Joy	Simplicity
Cooperation	Justice	Spirituality
Courage	Kindness	Sportsmanship
Creativity	Knowledge	Stewardship
Delight	Leadership	Success
Dignity	Learning	Teamwork
Diversity	Legacy	Thrift
Efficiency	Leisure	Time
Environment	Love	Tradition
Equality	Loyalty	Travel
Ethics	Making a difference	Trust
Excellence	Modesty	Truth

LESSON 7

Understanding Heart Characteristics, Part 2

This week, we will bring together a few concepts that intersect with our heart characteristics—wounds, maturity, and attachment styles.

Wounds

As we look at our heart characteristics, it is good to recognize that our heart characteristics create particularly sensitive spots within us. In Thrive training, we alternate looking for our heart characteristic with identifying our "main pain." If I have a heart characteristic of *justice for the weak*, then I will feel great pain when I see the strong take advantage of the weak. I might look at other people and wonder, "Why do they not see this terrible situation?" or perhaps I stay awake at night trying to think of ways to help. This is the beauty and the pain of heart characteristics—we are created to be like God in certain ways, and those ways are very good. When the evil of the world comes against the good of our heart, we feel pain. We can learn to look inside ourselves and say, "I am the kind of person who would feel pain in this situation. This is the way God created me, and it is good."[1] This recognition of our heart characteristics and the pain we feel is a step toward suffering well.

Maturity

Our maturity level affects how much we actually live from the heart characteristics God has placed within us. For instance, if God has gifted me with leadership but I am at child maturity and cannot take care of my needs as well as the needs of others, my leadership may look like bossiness and produce dissatisfaction in those I lead. My ability to manifest my gift of integrity will be affected by whether I've learned the child level task of doing hard things. The gift of contentment combined with infant maturity will look like laziness.

---

1 | Teaching from Jim Wilder.

As you pray about the heart characteristics God has given you, it is help-ful to look at the maturity tasks you are working to develop. How might your maturity gaps affect how your heart characteristic looks in your life?

Attachment Styles

Our attachment styles will also have an effect on how fully we express our heart characteristics. Perhaps God has given you the heart characteristic of kindness, but you currently have a dismissive attachment style. In dismissive attachment, one might not notice opportunities for kindness because you've learned to ignore or minimize emotional needs. As you heal from dismissive attachment, you may suddenly notice your kind heart is blooming as you see the emotions within you and in your friends. Or perhaps God has placed within you the heart characteristic of harmony, but you have disorganized at-tachment which brings disorder and conflict into your relationships. It might be difficult for you to recognize this characteristic of harmony within yourself until you begin to move toward a more secure attachment style.

If you know your attachment style, ask Jesus to reveal to you how that might be affecting your heart characteristic. Perhaps He can give you a glimpse of how your heart characteristic will be clearer as you move toward secure at-tachment.

Exercise

With this lesson, we will review Maribeth's contemplative outline "*Who am I?*"[2] where she shares some of her own ruminations with Immanuel as she sought to understand the person God created her to be. You might want to do a similar contemplative exercise with God, including some of the fol-lowing prompts from Maribeth's journaling:

"I am designed in the image of God!

I am one who is: _____

I value: _____

I believe people are: _____

I dislike it when: _____

Father, when I am _____, help me grow into the fullness of who I am so that I may continue to live out my true original design and true self with constancy!"

---

2 | Available for download at www.lifemodel.org/download/Who%20Am%20I.pdf

Download Maribeth's outline at the link in the footnote, read through it, and then create your own "Who Am I?" meditation to remind you of who you are when life pressures cause you to forget.

PONDER, JOURNAL, AND DISCUSS:

1. What heart characteristics seem to resonate with you the most?

2. Is there a type of painful situation that has seemed to bother you throughout your life? This thought may help you identify your heart characteristic.

3. What maturity tasks will you need to work on so you can more fully manifest your heart characteristic(s)?

4. How has your attachment style affected the expression of your heart characteristic(s)?

healing hearts
UNIT SIX

healing hearts
LESSON 1

Foundations for Processing Pain

In the world you will have tribulation, but take courage;
I have overcome the world. – John 16:33a NASB

Because we live in a very broken world, there is no option available in which we avoid pain altogether. Given this, one would think that the first order of business for parents of young children would be teaching them how to handle pain, but this doesn't seem to be in many parenting manuals—it's not a very popular topic. Because this topic is rarely on the parenting agenda, most of us learned to avoid acknowledging or feeling pain. This may work for a period of time, but most of us "hit the wall" by middle adulthood—we can no longer ignore our pain, the difficult emotions that accompany pain, or the relational damage that unprocessed pain has caused. Perhaps you are in this place now, or someone you love has reached this place. It's an excellent place to be, because pain is reality, and once we acknowledge its reality, we can begin to process our pain.

What does unprocessed pain look like? We often see the result of unprocessed pain in the things we do to *avoid* facing it. These might be any of the following (or your own personal favorite might be different!):[1]

Defending	Analysis/logic
Blaming	Electronics/social media
Staying busy	Television
Controlling	Alcohol and drugs
Enabling others	Unhealthy sexual activity

---

[1] Some material in this lesson is from Barbara Moon's book, *Reframing Your Hurts: Why You Don't Have to Fear Emotional Pain*, which is available on Amazon.com with her other excellent books. Barbara has been personally mentored by Jim Wilder for many years.

Walking on eggshells	Workaholism
Withdrawing	Thrill-seeking
Perfectionism	Food

There is a reason that the Bible so frequently says "Do not fear." Once we learn to process pain successfully, we won't fear it, and our lives expand with possibilities—no more avoided conversations, land mines in relationships, or unexplored dreams! Perhaps this is what is meant in Psalm 118:5 (NKJV)—"I called on the LORD in distress; The LORD answered me and set me in a **broad place**."

This broad place the Lord prepares for us is one where we face our pain together and without fear.

Setting a Good Foundation for Processing Pain

Our brains are designed to search for a solution for our pain. When we are in great emotional pain and distress, it's normal to feel like "I need to address this immediately! Help me NOW!" However, processing pain involves bringing pain to the surface, so we need to build our joy capacity before we dive into this process. If we don't focus on building a strong foundation of joy capacity prior to processing pain, we will find ourselves unable to face life with our pain exposed to the light.

How do we build joy capacity? Spend time with family members and friends building connection and joy—play games, take walks, watch joyful and/or funny movies or videos (YouTube has many videos of babies laughing, animals doing silly things, and bloopers from favorite shows or movies), build a fire outdoors and make S'mores, tell funny stories and clean jokes, look for free or inexpensive activities in your area, start a family hobby, have craft night—the ideas are endless.

QUIETING

The first relational skill we will use in processing pain is Quieting, which is an essential step in restoring our relational circuits. We must have our relational circuits on to gain access to Levels 3 and 4 of the brain, as these are the parts of the brain that can process pain. (We will talk more about the brain levels in a few weeks.)

Step 1: Shalom My Body. Jim Wilder designed these exercises to help quiet your body's reactions to distress (rapid breathing and heart rate, tense muscles, flushing, etc.:

- Moro Reflex, also called Breathe and Scrunch;
- Tapping by the collarbone;
- Deep breathing; and

- Yawning
- Each of these is accompanied by the phrase, "Whenever I am afraid, I will trust in You, O Lord" from Psalm 56:3.

Step 2: When you sense that your body is settled down, move on to *Appreciation*. Actively bring to mind one or more Appreciation Memories. When you can fully enter into your Appreciation Memories, you know your Relational Circuits have been restored.

Step 3: Connect to Immanuel. From your Appreciation Memory, ask Jesus, "What do you want me to know right now?" If you sense His presence or response, you are ready to begin processing the pain, or moving forward in the situation.

Don't worry if you need to quiet at times when you aren't able to take all these steps. It is a good idea to see which elements of Shalom My Body are most effective at quickly and unobtrusively quieting your body.

TRIGGERING

Unprocessed pain is stored in our subconscious mind as emotional sensations, so we are usually unaware when a current situation has "triggered" the recall of an unprocessed pain memory. When a current situation "feels" the same as the old, unprocessed pain memory, we will be triggered. For instance, Karl Lehman tells of how he found himself enraged at drivers who would race to the front of a merge lane in Chicago traffic, until he processed the pain of playground bullies pushing their way to the front of the line for the slide in elementary school. Once he processed the old pain, his emotional response became much more in line with the situation, and he was able to act like himself.

How do we know when we are triggered?

- Our response to a situation seems "over the top."
- We "feel" younger than we are.
- Feel like we don't have the resources to handle the situation.
- We respond with infant or child maturity.
- We feel or are incapable of acting like the person God created us to be.

What do we need when we are triggered? We need attunement–the sense that we are seen, heard, and valued.

PONDER, JOURNAL, AND DISCUSS:

1. Which of the ways to avoid pain described at the beginning of the lesson have you used most often in the past?

2. On a scale of 1 to 10, how much anxiety do you feel when you think about the following:[2]

Taking over a problem with:

____ My boss

____ My co-worker

____ My spouse

____ Other relative

The idea of:

____ Failure

____ Success

____ Emotional intimacy

____ Physical pain

____ Poor health/getting sick

____ Death

____ Wasting my life

The idea of:

____ Rejection by others

____ Work responsibilities

____ Family responsibilities

____ Abandonment

____ Exposure

____ God's view of me

____ God's will for me

____ Loss of control

____ Needs not being met

____ My own anger

____ Another person's anger

____ Shame

____ Making mistakes

3. What is a strong Appreciation Memory you can use to help you restore your relational circuits when they are dim or off? Name it below:

---

2 | Taken from exercise 11A in *Forming*, one of the Connexus video curriculum modules, available from Life Model Works. David Takle is the author of *Forming* and other books.

healing hearts
LESSON 2

Deepening My Connection to Jesus with Immanuel Journaling

As we move into healing our hearts, we will need more joy capacity as we discussed in Lesson 1. Our joy capacity grows as we deepen our connections with healthy people—in the moments of attunement, we are actually sharing their capacity. Deepening our connection with Immanuel enables us to tap into God's infinite capacity. Understanding this concept gives new meaning to the following verses:

> **Psalm 46:1** ESV God is our refuge and strength, a very present help in trouble.

> **Psalm 31:20** NASB You hide them in the secret place of Your presence from the conspiracies of man; You keep them secretly in a shelter from the strife of tongues.

> **Psalm 71:3a** NASB Be to me a rock of habitation to which I may continually come.

I love this image of God our Father, Jesus our brother, and Holy Spirit our guide, standing ready to welcome us, attune with us, and share their capacity with us. This is a much more relational picture of Immanuel than simply a fortress or rock to which we run to hide; this is a friend who is practicing active listening, validating and comforting our pain, and going with us to face our pain. I like to imagine an actual fortress during a medieval battle to which soldiers could return to receive rest after the turmoil outside the gates, medical care for their wounds, and the encouragement of their commanding officer that he will be with them as they return to the battle. This picture is worlds away from a distant Creator who watches our struggles from afar, judging our successes or failures.

Immanuel Journaling is one method of putting us in touch with God's attuned heart for us. *Joyful Journey* by Jim Wilder, John and Sungshim Loppnow, and Anna Kang, is the book that introduces Immanuel Journaling. This little book is a treasure!

Jim Wilder has stated that Immanuel Journaling has brought quicker transformation to more people than any other Life Model methodology introduce thus far. Consistent journaling with God with this framework places you in touch with God's heart for you—it enables you to receive His constant, abiding attunement with your emotions. As we learned last week, when we feel seen, heard, and understood, we are able to begin processing pain.

Immanuel Journaling is designed to deepen your attachment and connection to God who is with us. The importance of this is pointed out in a short blog post by Sungshim Loppnow below:

> "We become like the person we are most attached to. Think about this, who are you most attached to? This is likely the most important question you can ask yourself because you will become like that person over time.
>
> Immanuel Journaling is one tool, one simple way, that can help us attach to Jesus. To learn how to be bonded to Immanuel in a way that we begin to recognize that God is actually glad to be with us. He likes us and this attached relationship forms us.
>
> How are you arranging your life in such a way that the fruit flows from a bonded relationship with the gentle presence of God in Immanuel?"[1]

A steady practice of Immanuel Journaling will build your bond with Jesus so that you can more easily connect with Him to process pain, and so that He is an easily available resource throughout your day, which will help you process pain as it happens.

Immanuel Journaling is based on Exodus 3, the story of Moses at the burning bush. Notice the bolded words below:

> The LORD said, "**I have indeed seen** the misery of my people in Egypt. **I have heard them crying out** because of their slave drivers, and **I am concerned about their suffering.** So **I have come down to rescue them** from the hand of the Egyptians and to bring them up out of that land into a good and spacious land, a land flowing with milk and honey—the home of the Canaanites, Hittites, Amorites, Perizzites, Hivites and Jebusites. And now **the cry of the Israelites has reached me**, and **I have seen** the way the Egyptians are oppressing them. So now, go. **I am sending you** to Pharaoh to bring my people the Israelites out of Egypt."
>
> But Moses said to God, "Who am I that I should go to Pharaoh and bring the Israelites out of Egypt?"
>
> And God said, **"I will be with you."**

---

1 | www.presenceandpractice.com/post/relationship-is-key

Immanuel Journaling begins with Appreciation to ensure our relational circuits are on and then moves into hearing God speak to us in a pattern based on Exodus 3. The following provides a brief explanation of each step in Immanuel Journaling:

GRATITUDE

Dear God, I am thankful for... This can be anything; an event, being in nature, a pet, a special memory, or something that makes you smile.

My Dear child... Write what you think a loving father's response would be to your gratitude.

I CAN SEE YOU.

I can see you... Write what you believe God sees, what you think He observes in you. This can include physical sensations (breathing, pain, discomfort), emotions (tears, calm, relaxed) or what you are doing (sitting, tense body, restless).

I CAN HEAR YOU.

I can hear you... Write what you believe God hears you saying to yourself. This can be something simple like you saying that you enjoy the warmth of the morning sun or that you are frustrated with yourself or someone else.

I UNDERSTAND HOW BIG THIS IS FOR YOU, HOW YOU FEEL. I VALUE YOU.

I understand how... Write what you think God sees about your situation. Example: He sees how sad or overwhelmed you feel, what He enjoys about you as you enjoy the morning sun, etc.

I AM GLAD TO BE WITH YOU. I VIEW YOUR WEAKNESS TENDERLY.

I am glad to be with you. I... Write about what you perceive God might be saying to you in a kind, tender, loving, and gentle way.

I CAN DO SOMETHING ABOUT WHAT YOU ARE GOING THROUGH.

I can do something with you and for you... Write about what God might be saying as to how He will be with you and assist you.

READ YOUR RESULTS ALOUD, PREFERABLY TO ANOTHER PERSON.

You might be tempted to skip this step, but it's a very important part of the experience to hear the words you sensed from God out loud. If you have no one with whom you can share your journaling, read it out loud and let God's love and comfort sink into your soul.

PONDER, JOURNAL, AND DISCUSS:

1. This week, practice the Immanuel Journaling exercise, preferably with a friend or family member. Read your journaling to each other. Afterwards, take a minute or two to sit quietly together. If you do the Immanuel Journaling exercise alone, read your journaling to a friend as soon as possible.

2. Add these connection stories to your list of Appreciation Memories so you can return to them often.

healing hearts
LESSON 3

Helping Each Other Connect with Jesus

A common thread that is woven throughout the Journey Group experience is building stronger connections with both God and people. We've looked at how our community plays an integral part in our identity, our maturity, and our emotional growth. In this unit we are looking at emotional pain, and once again, our community is a key element of our healing.

In every area of life, relational connection helps us navigate challenges. Learning how to stay better connected with our friends and family is important, and now we will look at staying interactively connected with God throughout our days. This is called the Immanuel Lifestyle.

The Immanuel Lifestyle includes specific tools for connecting with Jesus like Immanuel Journaling and Immanuel Prayer. But most importantly, the Immanuel Lifestyle means developing the skills to live one's life constantly aware of the presence of Jesus and seeking His perspective in every situation. The relational skills we are learning in Journey Groups are all helpful in growing our capacity to stay connected to Jesus in ever more complex and distressing situations. Relational skills and the Immanuel Lifestyle go hand in hand.

Our ability to stay connected to God is often hindered by barriers that arise from past painful experiences. Because pain demands our attention, it's possible to become more driven to relieve pain than to build a secure connection with God. Immanuel Prayer encounters are designed to connect you with Jesus in a way that builds your secure bond with Him, and which frequently brings an element of pain relief.

"Immanuel Prayer is a process of connecting personally and interactively with the Lord, and removing barriers and hindrances to an intimate, interactive lifestyle of connection with him. The goal is to build and deepen a securely attached relationship with the Lord, one that increases our capacity to stay connected to him even in difficult life situations or painful experiences."[1]

With Immanuel Prayer, interactive connection is the primary goal rather than a secondary tool used to get somewhere else. This whole process is about experiencing relationship here and now, right in the midst of our joys and pains.

When we focus on interactive connection with God, we make some discoveries:

1. Healing is more likely to happen from a place of positive relational connection than from a place of pain.

2. The focus on interactive connection leads to repairs of the relational hindrances between us and God.

3. We can avoid the retraumatizing effects of reliving the pain while feeling alone and unconnected. We don't revisit the pain unless connection to Jesus is in place.

4. Jesus is allowed to guide the process of relational repair and healing of pain in the place of intimate connection with Him.

5. It is possible to help people who have difficulty connecting personally with the Lord by using guided Immanuel Prayer.

6. Having a guide present assists the recipient in building their connection with Immanuel so that they can connect well with Him on their own.

Patience is needed as we develop a strong connection with Immanuel. There is no limit to God's desire and intention to connect with us, and we may also be strongly motivated and intentional about this relationship. The need for patience arises from the fact that neural pathways take time to form and become a reliable "highway" for our connection with Him.

Imagine that each experience of connection creates a fragile strand of connection between us and God. With consistent repetition, these strands develop from threads into cords and from cords into strong cables. This analogy helps us understand that our ability to sense Him may be unstable. If we aren't intentionally consistent with practices that build relational connection, our neural pathways of connection will remain insubstantial and unpredictable.

God is constant and always reaching out to us, but our ability to sense Him fluctuates with our circumstances, health, moods, and other factors. This is one reason guided or accompanied Immanuel prayer encounters are so powerful.

---

1 | This definition comes from alivewell.org. Alive & Well provides Immanuel Encounter Guide training which will enable you to help others connect strongly to Jesus.

Another reason these encounters are effective is that they are consistent with our brain's design. Our brains change through authentic relationships with those who care about us. It is efficient, sensible, and beautiful to be accompanied into God's presence by a warm, loving, more experienced believer.

Building strong neural pathways to His presence through consistent, accompanied practice will bring you into an intimate, interactive lifestyle with Him.

The following *Connecting with Immanuel* exercise is one that is designed to be done as a guided experience. You can also use the exercise as a regular entry point for your personal times with Immanuel.

PONDER, JOURNAL, AND DISCUSS:

1. This week, practice the *Connecting with Immanuel* exercise with a friend or family member if at all possible. Make sure to share your connection stories. Afterwards, take a minute or two to sit quietly together.

2. Add these connection stories to your list of Appreciation Memories so you can return to them often.

CONNECTING WITH IMMANUEL[2]

1. **Heart Invitation**

   "Lord, I know You're here with me. Help me be aware of Your presence."

2. **Connect with the presence of the Lord.**

   Ask the Lord to bring to mind a time when you felt personally connected to Him, either through a direct interaction or a sense of deep appreciation for who He is or what He has done.

3. **Take time to re-experience that memory or moment of connection.**

   What happened? What did you see, sense, hear, feel, etc.?

   What was that experience like for you?

   What emotions were you feeling?

   Where in your body did you feel that?

   What did the Lord have for you in that experience?

4. **Refresh the connection in the present.**

   Express aloud to the Lord your appreciation for what you experienced in that connection until you have a sense of His presence with you now.

---

2 | Immanuel Encounter Guide Training, Alive and Well, Inc. alivewell.org

5. **Ask the Lord if there is more.**

   "Lord, I invite You to bring all You have for me right now."

6. **If you lose sense of the Lord's presence, return to the original connection.**

   Remind yourself of the concrete details of that experience until you feel again the sense of personal connection to the Lord or of deep appreciation.

7. **Share your connection experience with three other people.**

   Include details about what happened, your emotions and body, and what the Lord had for you there.

LESSON 4

Your Brain's Elevator

In *Rare Leadership*, Drs. Warner and Wilder picture the right hemisphere of our brain as an elevator, with each floor being a separate stage of processing our experiences. There are four sequential levels of brain function that move from the base of the brain to the top,[1] and one additional level that is the left hemisphere.

There are five steps to processing life's experiences, and these steps take us up through the four floors of the elevator, with the addition of the left hemisphere as the 5th floor. This brain elevator is different from any elevator you've ever experienced, however. As we ride this elevator, each trip is adding to the successful construction of the building.

The right hemisphere is designed by God to be the Control Center for our entire brain, so we'll take a look at the right hemisphere elevator in this unit. The right hemisphere operates more rapidly than the left hemisphere.

In addition, the right side is nonverbal, expressing itself mainly through eye contact, voice tone, facial expression, and body language. We store the emotional content of our memories (what it felt like emotionally) here, as well as what the memory felt like in our bodies. The right hemisphere doesn't store the narrative of our memories (what happened, when it happened, where we were, and who was with us).

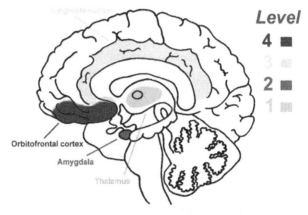

The Brain's Four Level Control Center

Level
4 ■
3 ▪
2 ■
1 ▪

Orbitofrontal cortex
Amygdala
Thalamus

---

1 | *Rare Leadership*, p. 66.

On each floor of the elevator, there are different tasks, feelings, and solutions, as illustrated in the chart below.[2]

LEVEL AND TASK	FEELING WHEN DISTRESSED	SOLUTION
Level 5: Articulate (Left hemisphere)	Confused: What is going on?	More information
Level 4: Act	Inadequate: I don't know what to do.	An Example
Level 3: Attune	Overwhelmed with my emotions	Mirroring/Attunement
Level 2: Assess	Disconnected from others; taking care of myself	Quieting
Level 1: Attach	Alone, rejected	The one I love

Over the next few weeks, we will learn more about the tasks of each floor, how pain manifests itself at the different levels, and what solutions and interventions are most helpful for each level. As you learn what tasks and solutions are needed at each level, you'll see where you need to focus in your journey to spiritual, relational, and emotional health.

Trauma interferes with successful movement up the elevator's levels. As we looked at in our Maturity Matters Unit, trauma can be described with two categories:

- **A Trauma** is the absence of the good things we need to flourish, such as loving attention and touch, security in the form of food, clothing, shelter, medical care, and assistance learning the maturity tasks.

- **B Traumas** are the bad things that happen to us, which can include major events like natural disasters, divorce, bullying, assault, deaths, or life-threatening illness in the family. Smaller events like a dog bite or getting lost in a store will be experienced as trauma if they overwhelm our capacity.

Both A and B Traumas can affect our Control Center at all levels, and as you can see from the center column in the chart above, trauma and pain cause different feelings at each level of the brain.

In a conversation with Jim Wilder some years ago, I expressed my surprise that my life seemed to have been greatly affected by the A Traumas I had experienced. Dr. Wilder responded, "Oh, over the years we have discovered that B Traumas don't always have a tremendous impact, but A Traumas **always**

2 | *Relational Skills in the Bible*, p. 112

cause long term damage, because A Traumas represent the absence of what you needed for your brain to fully develop." This insight has been a great comfort to me as I've walked through my healing—God is redeeming my pain and healing my brain in spite of an emotionally anemic childhood.

Here is a simple overview of the functions of Level One, the Attachment Center, as well as a description of what Level One needs from others to develop securely.

Level One – Attachment Center – Attach Securely

- Recognizes what is personal to me—people we know, familiar things, and locations, etc.

- Determines to what we will pay attention.

- Needs a secure relationship, someone who creates joy and quiet with me.

- Needs to be the sparkle in someone's eye—my brain knows someone is glad to be with me, which is JOY. (When we know someone is glad to be with us, the thalamus releases dopamine.)

- Is built through the first year of life, or can be created at any time later in life.

- Provides a secure foundation as we move through life.

- Even when we are not with "our person," we know we are secure.

When Level One is not well-developed, we will display insecure attachment. In the Heart-to-Heart Community Unit, we discussed the four attachment styles: Secure, Dismissive, Distracted, and Disorganized. (In the appendices, I've included Maribeth Poole's Attachment Profiles document so you can refresh your memory about the characteristics of each attachment style.)

Pain at Level One is attachment pain, which can be caused by a relational loss, or by the relational struggles which happen so frequently in a world where many people have insecure attachment styles.

Attachment pain lowers our capacity and makes all other forms of pain or distress worse. When we are in attachment pain, we may find ourselves more challenged in returning to joy from negative emotions, and the intensity of our emotions may be heightened. Because our brains want to avoid or relieve pain, be aware that we are more susceptible to cravings while in this level of pain. It's a good idea to avoid making major decisions while in attachment pain since many pain-reducing options are very appealing—new relationships, "treat yourself" purchases, changing jobs or locations, etc. Since attachment pain is very draining, getting plenty of rest is helpful as you are processing your pain.

It's important to know that attachment pain regarding the loss of a particular person can't be fixed by interactions with anyone else, which explains why "rebound" relationships rarely work. Attachment pain must be processed over time, and we will find that the pain and the healing comes in waves. We will feel the pain, get overwhelmed, and seek relief, desperate to avoid the feeling. We need a solution!

Initial Solution for Level One pain: Because Level One distress is at the very foundation of our identity, it's important to begin building secure bonds with a few friends or family members as you look at this pain. It can feel counterproductive to focus on sharing joy and quiet with a trusted friend or two when our brain is crying out for relief, but building your emotional capacity in this way will prepare you and your people to bear this load together.

PONDER, JOURNAL, AND DISCUSS:

Over the next few weeks, try to do the following Connect and Rest exercise at least 2-3 times a week with a friend or family member. This exercise helps build a more secure bond at Level One.

Connect and Rest (3 minutes for each round)

1. Set a timer for 3 minutes.

2. Sit knee to knee with your spouse or a good friend.

3. Make eye contact and smile genuinely. Imagine that someone has told you, "Using only your eyes, let this person know how you feel about them." If you do this exercise with someone you don't know as well, use your eyes to express "glad to be with you" joy.

4. Break eye contact and look down when you feel the need to break eye contact.

5. Continue with cycles of "connect" and "rest" for 3 minutes.

6. Variations on this exercise:

    ○ Think of an appreciation memory for 2 minutes before a round of Connect & Rest.

    ○ Tell each other a story from your day before a round of Connect & Rest.

    ○ Play some of your favorite music during Connect & Rest.

    ○ Quiet together for 2-5 minutes after a round of Connect & Rest.

    ○ Listen to Jesus for 5-10 minutes after a round of Connect & Rest, and share anything you journal or sense from God.

    ○ Connect and Rest can be played as a game with children. Explain it this way: "In this game, we are going to talk with only our eyes—

no words. We will look at each other and send the message, 'I like you and I'm glad to be with you' using only our eyes. When looking at each other starts to feel weird or uncomfortable, we look down at our lap and take a deep breath. When we feel ready, we look into each other's eyes again."

LESSON 5

Your Brain's Elevator: Levels Two & Three

As we move up through the brain's elevator, our focus and feelings change, but our goals are to stay connected to God and others, aware of the feelings of others, and to choose a solution that works for all involved. As we grow in our ability to stay securely connected with God and people, we will notice that these tasks are accomplished more often. We are becoming the people God created us to be in ever increasingly complex situations!

Another wonderful result of growth at each level is that we begin to respond differently to the weaknesses we notice in ourselves and others. We move away from our predator and possum ways and see more protector responses emerging.

Let's continue to examine our brain's elevator. When Level One determines that something is worthy of notice, the elevator moves to Level Two, where the situation is assessed. In the chart below, we see that Level Two's task is assessment, the feeling when distressed at Level Two is disconnection from others so that we feel like we need to take care of ourselves, and the solution for Level Two is the ability to quiet our feelings.

LEVEL AND TASK	FEELING WHEN	SOLUTION
Level 5: Articulate	Confused: What is going on?	More information
Level 4: Act	Inadequate: I don't know what to do.	An Example
Level 3: Attune	Overwhelmed with my emotions	Mirroring/Synchronizing
Level 2: Assess	Disconnected from others; taking care of myself	Quieting
Level 1: Attach	Alone, rejected	The one I love

Here is a simple overview of the functions of Level Two, the Assessment Center, as well as a description of what Level Two needs in order to recover from distress.

Level Two – Amygdala (Task: Assess for Safety)

- Assesses every situation for danger, provides us with adrenaline so we can take action.

- Level Two has only three opinions: Good, Bad, or Scary.

- Level Two generally takes one of 3 actions: Fight, Flight, Freeze. Self-protection is the goal.

- Level Two tends to be wired either for Approach or Avoid, based on past experience.

- When the brain is well trained, Level Two is able to quiet and pass on the information upward to Levels Three and Four for further action.

- Level Two is under the level of consciousness, faster than conscious thought.

- When poorly trained,
  - Level Two goes on high alert,
  - floods our system with adrenaline,
  - shuts down access to the upper levels, and
  - responds in a non-relational way.
  - Our "Little Red Guy" (amygdala) learns to stay on high alert, flooding our system with adrenaline (short term) and cortisol (long term stress hormone).
  - When Level Two is in control, we feel disconnected from others and like we must take care of ourselves. We are stuck in a non-relational state.

- The ability to quiet is so important that it has been called the best indicator of sound mental health.

Example of Level Two Fear: When "Fire" is yelled in a crowded theatre, the poorly trained Level Two will go into Fight or Flight mode. We will be unconcerned about the other people, and will push and shove until we reach safety. Only then will we calm down and remember that we are relational, and become concerned about other people's safety. A well-trained Level Two will pass on the message to Levels 3 and 4, and Level 4 will respond with relational, protective actions, such as offering help to those who need it, ensuring that everyone makes a safe exit. Level Two needs *quieting and will not respond to attunement.*

Level Two Solution: *Quieting*.

- Notice what your body feels like in various negative emotions.
- Notice what situations/people/events tend to create negative emotions for you.
- Set regular times to practice the Shalom My Body exercises. You want them to become second nature so that when your body begins to signal distress, you move quickly into deep breathing, yawning, tapping, etc.
- We learn quieting from other people who have the skill. Think of people you know who quiet themselves well. You can build this skill by simple observation and modeling your behavior on theirs.
- When you are with someone else who is upset at Level Two, take care of yourself first. Remember the advice given about oxygen masks in an airplane emergency, "Put your mask on first, then help the person with you." Take deep breaths, speak quietly, and move slowly.

Here is an overview of the functions of Level Three, the Assessment Center, as well as a description of what Level Three needs from others to recover.

Level Three: Cingulate Cortex — Synchronization Center (Task: Attune)

- Level Three is at the level of conscious thought, so it "knows" how it is feeling.
- Level Three is where negative emotions are processed, or NOT.
  - Sadness, Fear, Anger, Despair, Disgust, Shame
- A poorly trained Level Three will keep us stuck in negative emotions.
  - Because we get "stuck," we learn to avoid negative emotions we cannot process.
  - We will avoid situations in which we or others might have those negative emotions.
  - We develop a Fear Map of life: "Here are all the things I must avoid."
  - We drop down into Level Two very easily because emotions seem dangerous!
- A poorly trained Level Three has trouble both giving and receiving attunement.
  - We only learn what we have received.
  - Without a trained Level Three, we don't understand that we aren't attuning, and

- ○ We don't understand why others are so upset.

- ○ We don't hold on to the attunement we receive because we go into another negative emotion so quickly, and

- ○ We feel overwhelmed with our emotions.

- Not only does this part of the brain synchronize many brain processes, but it synchronizes us with other people and with our world.

- A well-trained Level Three can both give and receive attunement.

- When we have someone to attune and synchronize with us in each negative emotion, we learn our pathway back to joy in the negative emotion.

  - ○ Fear
  - ○ Anger
  - ○ Sadness
  - ○ Shame
  - ○ Despair
  - ○ Disgust

- A well-trained Level Three can return to joy (being glad to be with you), even in a negative emotion.

- It may hear words, but it BELIEVES non-verbal communication.

Example of Level Three Fear: My daughter Livy and I were at dinner with one of her friends. Livy and I were discussing something with a tiny bit of heat. The friend told us, "I'm really nervous—y'all need to stop talking about this! I can't handle it!" Her Level Three was unable to handle even the perception that we were angry. We attuned with her fear, quieted with her, and continued our conversation with less intensity so that she could stay connected and relational. Level Three needs *attunement, so Level Three upset says,* "Show *me you understand!*"

Level Three Solution: *Attunement/Synchronization.*

- Dr. Daniel Siegel uses the phrase "Name it to tame it" with regard to Level Three.[1] As you observe and notice what emotions you are feeling, you are attuning with yourself.

- After you have noticed and named your emotions, allow yourself to feel them and share them with someone trustworthy who is a peaceful presence. Allow that person to attune with you, and you will likely find the intensity of your emotion lessening.

- There is a subtle difference between simply sharing your feelings and

---

1 | Dr. Siegel has written *Parenting from the Inside Out, The Whole-Brained Child, No Drama Discipline,* and a number of other books. "Name it to tame it" is from *The Whole-Brained Child.*

amplifying distress. In sharing, we want to be understood. In amplifying, we want to stir up emotion in the listener as well. As a recovering "amplifier," I can say that the need to amplify distress likely comes from some unhealed pain and as you grow in your joy capacity, you may want to do Immanuel Journaling or seek facilitated Immanuel Prayer to help you process that pain.

- When you are with someone else who is upset at Level Three, validation and comfort are two ways to offer attunement:
  - *Validation* means we identify how they are feeling and how big it is to them: "You are really mad—I can see how upset you are." Validation does NOT mean we have to agree with how they feel, nor do we have to feel the same way. We want to acknowledge their feelings.
  - To offer *comfort* is to let someone know they are not alone in the situation. "I'm so sorry you are going through this. This is a tough thing to face." This is not a time to offer solutions unless they are requested.
  - When you've offered validation and comfort, you may want to ask, "What would you like me to do?" Offering some options is a good way to set boundaries for yourself while still offering help. You might say something like this:
    » "Would you like me to listen? To pray with you? To offer advice? To think of some resources that might help?"
    » Don't offer more than you can give, and when they tell you what they'd like, give them only what they request.

PONDER, JOURNAL, AND DISCUSS:

1. Can you think of a time when you were in Level Two distress? Do you think you felt the situation was "bad" (creating anger) or "scary" (creating fear)? Did you go into a "fight," "flight," or "freeze" response? Were you able to quiet?

2. The negative emotions we process at Level Three are fear, anger, sadness, shame, disgust, and despair. Can you think of a time when you felt one of these and someone attuned with you? Did they offer a form of validation and comfort? What did you feel like in your emotions when you realized they saw how you felt? In your body?

3. What would be different in our society if parents were taught how to help their young children quiet Level Two distress? What about Level Three upset? What evidence do you see around you that these skills are lacking? What might be some creative ways to make changes in your sphere of influence? In society at large?

LESSON 6

Your Brain's Elevator Levels Four & Five

In Levels One, Two, and Three of the brain's elevator, our brain is working hard to recognize what is personal to us (Level One) and hold on to our pattern of attachment, to evaluate whether we are in danger (Level Two), and to stay connected to other people and the situation (Level Three). Now, at Level Four, we are looking for a solution to the problem that is satisfying, one that enables us to be the person God created us to be. Level Four leads us to act, and we need a good example at this level.

LEVEL AND TASK	FEELING WHEN	SOLUTION
Level 5: Articulate	Confused: What is going on?	More information
Level 4: Act	Inadequate: I don't know what to do.	An Example
Level 3: Attune	Overwhelmed with my emotions	Mirroring/Synchronizing
Level 2: Assess	Disconnected from others; taking care of myself	Quieting
Level 1: Attach	Alone, rejected	The one I love

Here is a simple overview of the functions of Level Four, the Identity Center, as well as a description of what Level Four needs when in distress.

Tasks Performed by Level Four – The Captain – Identity Center – Act

- A well-trained Level Four remembers our true identity (the person God created you to be).

- It reminds us "what it is like us and our people" to do in this situation.
- It has an individual as well as a group identity.
- It can override Level 2 upset.
  ○ "Thanks for the warning, we can take it from here."
  ○ It can stay relational, even when things are going wrong.
  ○ It recognizes our part of the problem–"Oh, I see how I upset you. I'm so sorry."
  ○ It is creative and flexible, and it comes up with great, satisfying solutions to problems.

PAIN AT LEVEL FOUR LEAVES US FEELING INADEQUATE.

- A poorly trained Identity Center leaves us unsure of what to do in various situations.
  ○ We feel inadequate.
  ○ We don't know what it is like us and our people to do.
  ○ We can't see our part in the problem.
    » "If YOU would only straighten up, this would all be okay."
  ○ We are rigid and not creative—we can only think of OUR solution to the problem.
    » We shut down every solution others offer us.
  ○ When we lose connection at Level Four, we drop down into Level Three upset and maybe even Level Two alarm and Level One despair at being all alone.
- We don't understand the meaning of the situation; "Am I a terrible person? Is God not with me?"
- We feel inadequate and as if we don't have enough resources.

SOLUTIONS AT LEVEL FOUR: EXAMPLES AND STORIES

Level Four distress leave us feeling inadequate, unsure of who we are and what actions we should take. The most effective solution at Level Four is an example, whether in real time or in the form of a story. When we tell our children stories about mistakes we have made and how we handled them, we are providing them with Level Four examples. When we read in Scripture of Moses' humility, Abraham's faith, Job's refusal to curse God, Jesus' advice to His disciples, and the stories of the Acts of the Apostles, God is graciously providing us with examples through stories.

Sharing *Acting Like Myself* stories with our families and friends is a key way of growing our Identity Center at Level Four. As Chris Coursey says in the Track 2 online course,

> "Acting like myself stories are stories where the focus shifts from *sharing the emotion* [as we do in a Return to Joy Story] to describing *what it is like me and my people to do* in the middle of distress. I discover how to be myself when I feel a certain emotion. Have you ever encountered someone who, when upset, responded in a way that was relational, friendly and kind in spite of their upset? What about the opposite response? Have you experienced someone who was hurtful, mean or frightening when they were upset? What is the difference between the two examples in terms of how it feels to be around someone when they're upset?"[1]

When our Level Four is poorly trained, we are most concerned with relief from negative emotions. As we mature, we will find ourselves shifting to "How can I act like the person God created me to be?" We are also more in touch with how to express our unique personality and gifts in a given situation.

Example of Level Four distress: Joanne and Lisa have an unresolved disagreement, and Joanne feels very sad, but she has no idea how to repair this rupture. Joanne asks her more mature friend Marcia, "How have you handled this type of situation in the past?" and Marcia shares some experiences of relational repair from her own life.

After an experience moves up through the elevator Levels One through Four, our experience crosses over to the left hemisphere, which we also call Level Five. Here is an overview of the left hemisphere/Level Five functions as well as a description of what Level Five needs when in distress.

Level Five: The Left Side of the Brain

- Acts as a Library or File Cabinet in that it stores information,
- Stores the content of the memory, the story of "what happened,"
- Adds the verbal content to our interactions,
- Slower than the Right Hemisphere (i.e., Information and Verbal Input is processed more slowly than Emotion and Non-verbal Input),
- Makes sense and gives meaning to our experiences when Levels One through Four have processed our experiences.

---

1 | THRIVEtoday Relational Skills Training handbook, p. 97.

PAIN AT LEVEL FIVE LEAVES US FEELING CONFUSED.

- We don't have the information we need to take action.
- This is not a highly emotional state of upset.
- We feel confused and unsure of the meaning of a situation.

Example of Level Five Distress: "Why is there one shoe on the side of the highway? How does that happen?"

Level Five is the only level at which information provides a satisfying solution to our distress. Have you had the experience of being upset and having friends quote Scripture to you? Did you feel angry or sad that your friends didn't feel your pain with you? Perhaps you felt also felt sad or guilty that the Word was not a comfort to you. It's possible that you (like I) have been surprised when you offered Scripture or advice and were rebuffed. Understanding how pain is processed will help us know what we need when we are upset and how to offer a satisfying response when others are upset.

Another task at Level Five is attributing meaning to an experience. God-sight means that He is always willing to share His perspective so we can attune with His viewpoint. Our *sark* or flesh has a perspective that is always at odds with God, so when our sark is combined with painfully unprocessed events in our life, our perspective is skewed. This skewed perspective leads to a faulty view of ourselves and others.

Chris Coursey talks about this false sense of self in the Track 2 preparation:

> "We can have a false self that is based on faulty explanations about who we are. This is the conflict that goes on at Level Five. It means who we feel like we are internally does not match what we know about God's truth and what Scripture tells us about being recipients of God's love and favor through Jesus Christ.
>
> Paul tells us in Roman 8:1, *There is therefore now no condemnation to those who are in Christ Jesus, who do not walk according to the flesh, but according to the Spirit.* NKJV
>
> This is a breath of fresh air if we are used to feeling beat up by the sark in the form of condemnation by others, accused, rejected, humiliated, threatened, slandered and more. We tend to remember these moments clearly, in particular our left hemisphere explanations, and the scars can run deep. There are always good reasons the distortions are present in the first place. Because our brain is designed to function in peace, we need to constantly invite Jesus to correct lies and distortions.
>
> Do you recognize any distortions about yourself that need to be corrected?"[2]

---

2 | Ibid., p. 96

As you identify distortions you have believed, take time to talk with Immanuel about these distortions and to get His perspective about your identity.

The solutions to distress at Level Five are correct information and God's perspective to correct distorted identities and beliefs we've received from our own sark or that of others. Correcting the sark is a lifelong journey of intimacy with Jesus, updating our mindsight with His perfect understanding.

We have now looked at the elevator in your brain and examined what happens at each level as we process our life experiences, whether joyful or traumatic.

PONDER, JOURNAL, AND DISCUSS:

1. It is always good for us to look at where we have strengths and weaknesses. Awareness of our gaps will prevent us from being caught off guard by triggering and allows us to prepare for potentially problematic situations. When Level Four is triggered and in distress, we find it hard to act like our truest self. In which of the following situations would you be most able to behave out of your true identity, and in which situation would you have a difficult time being your true self:

   ○ You are explaining something to a group of friends, and one of your friends tells you that you are *wrong*.

   ○ You say something to a friend, and she tells you that you hurt her feelings.

   ○ You are in a group, and they start gossiping about someone you know.

   If you identify one of these situations where you might run into relational trouble, ask Jesus about it. "Jesus, what do you want me to know about this? How would you guide me to handle an interaction like this?"

2. When you are struggling to understanding God's perspective in a situation, you may want to invite a friend to help you connect with Jesus about the situation. Based on what you've learned in this unit, what benefits might you receive from this solution?

APPENDICES

APPENDIX 1
Maturity Indicators

THE INFANT STAGE: BIRTH THROUGH AGE 3

Newborns and toddlers are included here, up to the age where they can effectively say what their needs are.

PRIMARY TASK to be completed during this stage: **Learning to receive.**

PRIMARY RESULTING PROBLEM in adult life when this task is not completed: **Weak or stormy relationships.**

If our primary dependency needs are not met, we will spend the rest of our lives trying to get others to take care of us.

PERSONAL TASKS	COMMUNITY AND FAMILY TASKS	WHEN THE TASKS FAIL
1. Lives in joy: Expands capacity for joy, learns that joy is one's normal state, and builds joy strength.	Parents delight in the infant's wonderful and unique existence.	Weak identity; fear and coldness dominate bonds with others.
2. Develops trust.	Parents build strong, loving bonds with the infant—bonds of unconditional love.	Has difficulty bonding, which often leads to manipulative, self-centered, isolated, or discontented personality.
3. Learns how to receive.	Gives care that matches the infants needs without the infant asking.	Is withdrawn, disengaged, self-stimulating, and unresponsive.
4. Begins to organize self into a person through relationships.	Discovers true characteristics of the infant's unique identity through attention to the child's behavior and character.	Has an inability to regulate emotions.
5. Learns how to return to joy from every unpleasant emotion.	Provides enough safety and companionship during difficulties, so the infant can return to joy from any other emotion.	Has uncontrollable emotional outbursts, excessive worry and depression. Avoids or gets stuck in certain emotions.

CHARACTERISTICS OF "ADULT INFANTS"

Adult infants who have not received in these important areas as babies, will always be needy as adults.

- They will not be able to take care of themselves emotionally nor will they be able to appropriately receive important things from others.

- Adult infants will not ask for what they need because they believe if others really cared for them, they would figure out what they needed.

- Adult infants cannot handle criticism even if it is valid and constructive, because they see any negative feedback as a personal attack.

- Adult infants are often possessive of relationships, territory, power, and possessions.

- Adult infants use fear bonding to ensure others will stay bonded to them.

- Although "high functioning" adult infants can appear responsible in many areas, like handling personal finances and being punctual and reliable, emotionally they are severely crippled making it difficult for them to have successful and enduring relationships.

THE CHILD STAGE: AGE 4 THROUGH 12

Transition from infant stage to child stage is marked by the child being able to say what is needed. Age 12 is the earliest age this stage can be completed.

PRIMARY TASK to be completed during this stage: **Taking care of self.**

PRIMARY RESULTING PROBLEM in an adult life when this task is not completed: **Not taking responsibility for self.**

"Child adults" can take care of themselves but they can only take care of themselves often at the expense of others.

PERSONAL TASKS	COMMUNITY AND FAMILY TASKS	WHEN THE TASKS FAIL
1. Asks for what is needed; can say what one thinks and feels.	Teaches and allows child to appropriately articulate needs.	Experiences continual frustration/disappointment because needs are not met. Often passive aggressive.

2. Learns what brings personal satisfaction.	Helps child to evaluate consequences of own behaviors and to identify what satisfies self.	Is obsessed with or addicted to food, drugs, sex, money, and power in a desperate chase to find satisfaction.
3. Develops enough persistence to do hard things.	Challenges and encourages child to do difficult tasks child does not feel like doing.	Experiences failure, remains stuck and undependable, is consumed with comfort and fantasy life.
4. Develops personal resources and talents.	Provides opportunities to develop child's unique talents and interests.	Fills life with unproductive activities despite God given abilities.
5. Knows self and takes responsibility to make self understandable to others.	Guides in discovering the unique characteristics of the child's heart.	Fails to develop true identity; conforms to outside influences that misshape identity.
6. Understands how he or she fits into history as well as the "big picture" of what life is about.	Educates the child about the family history as well as the history of the family of God.	Feels disconnected from history and is unable to protect self from family lies or dysfunctions that are handed down.

"Child adults" who have adult bodies but are emotionally at the child level of maturity will always appear ego-centric.

Taking care of self includes the ability to push through on difficult tasks. This requires developing patience and persistence and takes some guidance. Unfortunately for all, there is a current "entitlement" trend in America. It erroneously suggests that if you are worthwhile, you will not have to do hard things. *This misconception goes against all conventional wisdom and severely limits the development of maturity.*

THE ADULT STAGE: AGE 13 TO BIRTH OF 1ST CHILD

Age 13 is about the earliest age at which adult-level tasks may be accomplished.

PRIMARY TASK to be completed during this stage: **Taking care of two people simultaneously.**

PRIMARY RESULTING PROBLEM when this task is not completed: **Lacks the capacity to be in mutually satisfying relationships.**

You will know when a person has graduated from the child level of maturity to the adult level because he will shift from being a self-centered child to a both-centered adult. While a child needs to learn me-centered fairness (how do I make it fair for me), an adult learns we-centered fairness (how do I make it fair for us). Mutuality is the trademark of an adult because he can take care of two people at the same time.

PERSONAL TASKS	COMMUNITY AND FAMILY TASKS	WHEN THE TASKS FAIL
1. Cares for self and others simultaneously in mutually satisfying relationships.	Provides the chance to participate in group life.	Is self-centered, leaves others dissatisfied and frustrated.
2. Remains stable in difficult situations and knows how to return self and others to joy.	Affirms that the young adult will make it through difficult times.	Conforms to peer pressure and participates in negative and destructive group activities.
3. Bonds with peers; develops group identity.	Provides positive environment/activities where peers can bond	A loner with tendencies to isolate; excessive self importance.
4. Takes responsibility for how personal actions affect others including protecting others from self.	Teaches young adults that their behaviors impact others and impact history.	Is controlling, harmful, blaming, and unprotective to others.
5. Contributes to the community; articulates "who we are" as part of belonging to the community.	Provides opportunities to be involved in important community tasks.	Does not become a life-giving contributor to the community; is self-absorbed and uses others—drains society.
6. Expresses the characteristics of his or her heart in a deepening personal style.	Holds the person accountable while still accepting and affirming the aspects of his or her true self.	Is driven to 'play roles,' prove self to the world, get results, and seek approval.

When people with adult bodies are functioning below the adult level of maturity, you will know because, in the end, your interactions with them will never feel mutual. You will go away feeling like in order to maintain a relationship with them you will always need to give more, listen more, or tolerate more than they would ever be willing to do for you.

Adults know how to remain stable in difficult situations and can return self and others to joy. People who cannot do this will either avoid, escape, or get stuck in certain emotions, crippling many of their endeavors and relationships. For example, if I avoid all anger, it eventually explodes into rage. If I get stuck in shame and failure, I may become depressed or even suicidal. And if I escape pain and rejection by doing drugs or having a sordid affair, I've only increased my misery and suffering.

THE PARENT STAGE: BIRTH OF 1ST CHILD UNTIL YOUNGEST CHILD HAS BECOME AN ADULT

PRIMARY TASK to be completed during this stage: **Sacrificially taking care of children.**

PRIMARY RESULTING PROBLEM when this task is not completed: **Distant or conflicted family relationships.**

You know you are at the parent stage when you can sacrificially care for your children without resenting the sacrifice or expecting to receive anything for your efforts. You may feel exhausted or overwhelmed at times, but you still will be able to appreciate, not begrudge, your sacrifice.

PERSONAL TASKS	COMMUNITY AND FAMILY TASKS	WHEN THE TASKS FAIL
1. Protects, serves, and enjoys one's family.	The community gives the opportunity for both parents to sacrificially contribute to their family.	Family members are (1) at risk, (2) deprived, and (3) feel worthless or unimportant.
2. Is devoted to taking care of children without expecting to be taken care of by the children in return.	The community promotes devoted parenting.	Children have to care for parents, which is impossible and leads to child abuse/neglect and/or "parentified" children which blocks instead of facilitates their maturity.
3. Allows and provides spiritual parents and siblings for their children.	The community encourages relationships between children and extended spiritual family members.	Children are vulnerable to peer pressure, to cults, to any misfortune, and are less likely to succeed in life's goals. Parents get overwhelmed without extended family support.

4. Learns how to bring children through difficult times and return to joy from other emotions.	The community supports parents by giving them encouragement, guidance, breaks, and opportunities to recharge.	Hopeless, depressed, disintegrating family units develop.

- Entitlement philosophy pervades modern parenting. "I'm entitled to do all the things I was doing as an adult, and I should not have to make any sacrifices of time, money, or social activities." Do not misunderstand. Parenting does involve sacrifice, but it is not about giving up who you are, but about becoming who you are!

- It is vitally important for parents to learn how to **protect**, **serve**, and **enjoy** their families for all members to be fulfilled. Balancing all three requires community support and elder guidance.

- Mature parents are aware that they cannot provide everything their children will need and allow opportunities for others to come alongside the child.

- In the end, mature parenting is about representing God to one's family. When you accomplish that, you are ready to graduate to the final level of maturity.

THE ELDER STAGE: BEGINNING WHEN YOUNGEST CHILD HAS BECOME AN ADULT

PRIMARY TASK to be completed during this stage: **Sacrificially taking care of the community.**

PRIMARY RESULTING PROBLEM when this task is not completed: **The overall maturity of the community declines.**

Most in our culture never make it to this level of maturity. This is unfortunate because the success of any country, community, school, or church body will have a direct correlation to the presence of true elders who are guiding and advising.

PERSONAL TASKS	COMMUNITY AND FAMILY TASKS	WHEN THE TASKS FAIL
1. Establishes an accurate community identity and acts like self in the midst of difficulty.	The community recognizes elders in the community.	There is meaninglessness, disorder, loss of direction, and disintegration of all social structures from government to family.

2. Prizes each community member and enjoys the true self in each individual looking past their flaws and facades to see the persons they have been designed to be.	The community provides opportunities for elders to be involved with those in all of the other maturity stages.	Life-giving interactions diminish along with life giving interdependence stunting the community's growth. Fragile, at-risk people fail to heal or survive.
3. Parents and matures the community.	The community creates a structure to help the elders do their job which allows people at every stage of maturity to interact properly with those in other stages and to listen to the wisdom of maturity.	When elders do not lead, unqualified people do, resulting in immature interactions at every level of the community.
4. Gives life to those without a family through spiritual adoption.	Places a high value on being a spiritual family to those with no family.	When the "familyless" are not individually taken care of, poverty, violence, crisis, crime, and mental disorders increase.

- True elders establish an accurate community identity by finding out what their community has been designed by God to be, rather than imposing what they would like it to be.

- True elders can act like themselves in the midst of difficulty.

- True elders can handle criticism and rejection, speak the truth in love even when it is not easy or popular, serve without being appreciated, encourage needed growth and change, delight in younger people's skill and power, and place what is best for the community over personal fairness or preference

APPENDIX 2
Journaling About Your Relationship

Journaling about my relationship. You can journal fairly quick answers to these questions, or you can take one set of questions per day and journal your thoughts more in-depth. Both can provide great insights.

Do I increase his/her joy? Does he/she increase my joy? How could we grow in this area? Jesus, what are You saying?

Do we quiet together well? How could we practice this skill in a natural way? Jesus, what do You want me to know?

Do I see fear bonds in the relationship? Jesus, what do You want me to know? What are baby steps to growing out of this fear bond? What will this relationship look like when we are joy/love bonded?

Do I attune well with him/her? Does he/she attune well with me? What can we do to grow our understanding and ability to synchronize with each other's emotions, thoughts, hopes, and dreams? Jesus, please share Your thoughts with me.

What are our respective attachment styles? How does this create difficulties? How does this work well for us? Jesus, show me what secure attachment will look like for us.

What are some of my heart values? His/hers? How does this affect our different perspectives on life? Jesus, help me see the heart values You put in this person and in me.

What is my current approximate maturity level? What is his/hers? How does this affect our ability to stay relational and connected in difficult times?

APPENDIX 3
Attachment Profiles

I. "SALLY SECURE"	II. "DISMISSIVE DANNY"	III. "AMBIVALENT ARNOLD"	IV. "DISORGANIZED DEBBIE"
Secure/Autonomous Attachments Secure Parents	Avoidant Attachments Dismissive Parents	Resistant or Ambivalent Attachments Pre-Occupied or Entangled Parents	Disorganized/Disoriented Attachments Unresolved/Disorganizing Parents
Due to knowing well that God is all He claims to be, Sally has confidence as she goes through life. She is looking forward to the "adventures" that are to come. She is not fearful of the mistakes she will make as she relates to her family, friends, co-workers, and others. Sally is not unnerved by the many things she must learn, she is a non-defensive and eager learner. At the times when interpersonal conflict arises, Sally does not withdraw in fear or become angry and demanding. Instead, she interacts with the person, pursuing mutual care and respect if at all possible. Sally is able to draw out the struggles another person is having, reflectively showing her understanding as she joins them in the path that lies ahead.	Danny lives with a focus on following rules. Since he has not developed an inner confidence in handling hard situations, he feels a need to have clear guidelines to follow. This becomes more important to him than entering into the emotional pain or disturbances occurring with those he meets. Danny's creativity and ability to problem solve are limited due to his main focus on following rules. It is fearful for Danny to let people have possible negative opinions of him. Thus, he is motivated and guided by a strong shame focus. He is defensive when problems occur and afraid he may be found "wanting." This inhibits his capability to learn. Due to his need to keep life seemingly in control, Danny is not able to enter fully into a difficult situation. To do this, he must dismiss or minimize the full significance of what he or others are experiencing.	Arnold has a strong desire to relate well and care about those in his life. Whichever person or event is the most demanding is the one that grabs his attention. He lives with "the squeaky wheel gets the oil" syndrome. People do know they are important to Arnold when a crisis occurs, but if nothing urgent is being presented to Arnold, they may not know his true response. Due to the crises of the moment, responsibilities often are not taken care of, which results in frustration with him by others. When Arnold has a need in his own life, he is distracted from his life responsibilities as he seeks someone to meet his need. When he has found someone, he tends to become overly dependent for a period of time, being paralyzed and not functioning as he wishes. Arnold has a secret. Although he feels guilty and has tried repeatedly to stop, he continues to be drawn to pornography. He tries to remind himself that he will hate himself later, but the urge for the personal excitement, both physically and emotionally, is stronger than his self discipline. The days most barren of personal affirmation and tenderness are the ones he most often gives in to his addiction. Arnold's life is governed by chaos more than by his values and goals.	At first, Debbie appears to be a stable, reliable, and responsible colleague. This is the case until difficult situations arise and she emotionally disintegrates. As time goes on, Debbie's life is increasingly characterized by emotional outbursts and chaos. It seems like she has an internal magnet to fearful situations, as she is constantly in the middle of whatever crisis is at hand. In situations that are threatening to her, she is unable to gain a realistic perspective, bringing herself to a sense of calm. Instead, she is quite reactive. She is not easily able to receive the help she needs, and cannot relate in a way that is helpful to others. Verbal reassurance does her no good. She loses focus of her personal preferences and values during the times she is disoriented and internally disorganized.

I. "SALLY SECURE"	II. "DISMISSIVE DANNY"	III. "AMBIVALENT ARNOLD"	IV. "DISORGANIZED DEBBIE"
Secure/Autonomous Attachments Secure Parents	Avoidant Attachments Dismissive Parents	Resistant or Ambivalent Attachments Pre-Occupied or Entangled Parents	Disorganized/Disoriented Attachments Unresolved/Disorganizing Parents
Sally Secure grew up in an atmosphere in which her parents were finely tuned in to her physical and emotional needs, giving timely responses. She was encouraged to express her thoughts and opinions and talk about the hard times that came in growing up. Her parents stayed involved, helping her learn to voice her needs, receive help as needed, take care of herself, empathize and appropriately care for others. Sally was encouraged to try new things and could do so with confidence due to the secure base in life provided by her family. Her family's environment set the stage for her to be able to return to joy from any situation or emotion. As she grew, Sally learned what brought her personal satisfaction and joy. She had opportunities provided to her in which she could learn of the power given to her by God to bring life to others.	Danny quickly learned the rule that "children are to be seen and not heard." Of course, he was just a child, so what did he know? Danny did not experience the faces of his parents lighting up in the delight of who he was. His emotions were dismissed as being unimportant and "incorrect." The significance of his needs was not recognized and often went unmet. At times, he learned that his need presented an inconvenience to his parents and if he wanted to avoid the pain of being ignored or shamed, he must not let it be known. Although he did want to be loved and given attention, he learned not to expect it or seek it. He knew that his needs, opinions, feelings, and desires were unimportant. In order to navigate in his world, Danny focused on being a good child. He appeared to be well adjusted since he did not voice complaints or appear to be a clingy child. This "getting it right" added to the cycle of not receiving focused attention. There was no need to be met and no behavioral problem to be disciplined. This inflexible and non-spontaneous pattern led him into the path of a rigid relational style.	Arnold's parents truly desired to give their child the attention and love needed; yet they were often distracted from doing so by other issues in life that riveted their emotional attention. Whatever situation had the most emotional intensity determined their focus. This inconsistency in availability, sensitivity, perceptivity and effectiveness left Arnold with a sense of uncertainty, giving him an urgent and constant need for comfort from external interactions. At times, his parents remembered their desire to love their child without tuning in to his specific needs at the time. This lack of sensitivity resulted in emotionally engulfing Arnold. He felt overwhelmed and anxious regarding future interactions. Internally Arnold was consumed with and driven by emotional doubts of one form or another. (Am I loved? Will the person leave me? Am I going to be rejected? Will their need to love me drown my needs for timely synchronization?) Along with this undercurrent, Arnold was a very caring child who gravitated to the "underdogs" and he received great appreciation from those he helped. He learned this was a great way to receive the attention he craved.	Disorganized Debbie grew up in a home fraught with fear. The parents to whom she needed to go for security were the very ones who brought her fear. Her mother was a very anxious lady whose emotions flowed out to her children when she related to them. She was constantly certain that danger was lurking, their house would be broken into, Dad was hurt in an accident if he was late getting home from work, and the children would get hurt when they played and climbed. Debbie learned from her mother that the world is not a safe place to live. Debbie also lived in terror of her father coming home at the end of each day. Would he fly into a rage? Was tonight the night that he would enter her bedroom and violate her? Would he again smash mom against the wall? Yes, it is certain to Debbie that the world is unsafe, not organized or reliable, and will not offer her love and protection.

210

I. "SALLY SECURE"	II. "DISMISSIVE DANNY"	III. "AMBIVALENT ARNOLD"	IV. "DISORGANIZED DEBBIE"
Secure/Autonomous Attachments Secure Parents	Avoidant Attachments Dismissive Parents	Resistant or Ambivalent Attachments Pre-Occupied or Entangled Parents	Disorganized/Disoriented Attachments Unresolved/Disorganizing Parents
Sally Secure grew up with a sense of confidence and freedom to explore her world. She has enough inner certainty to tackle challenges in life in ways that are satisfactory to her. When emotional challenges as well as joyful times arise, she is able to fully feel the emotions while continuing to live from a kindly and respectful relational stance. She knows how to relate empathically with others and interact in ways that repair relationships when they "rupture." Sally is not as concerned with "fairness" as she is with bringing about mutual care and the best interest of "her people." Sally responded with ease regarding her childhood and talked objectively. She was able to see both the negative and positive influences of her parents. Her fluid speech and self-reflection show access to memories that corroborated her life story.	Danny grew up in an environment in which his needs, emotions, opinions, and ideas were disregarded. His mind internalized the belief of being unimportant and later, he could not easily recognize his own value. Memories are "recorded" through a process that includes emotional "wiring." Not getting the message that who he is and what he thinks is of any importance laid the groundwork for life's events not to be "logged" well in his memory. Thus Danny has a limited view of himself. His life awareness is limited to "non-emotional" domains. Spontaneous and creative thinking has been discouraged, resulting in his interpersonal relationships being stilted. Danny's view of life is inflexible as he takes a restrictive approach to living in the world. Danny did not have much memory recall as questions were posed to him. He could not reflect on how his childhood relationships made an impact on who he is in the present. He would give an overall opinion of his childhood and parents, but was not able to give specific examples to corroborate the impressions of his life story.	Arnold recognized the importance of love and giving care, and he was driven to be a "caregiver." He had been conditioned as he grew to focus on the emotionally demanding situations in life, and thus his mind tracked these types of situations. He learned to attach to emotional crises more than to people. This resulted in his being "off and on" in relationships, depending on the emotional intensity of the moment. His preoccupation with demanding situations resulted in his being unreliable relationally as well as with day-to-day responsibilities. Arnold's insecurity played out with him demanding the spotlight, being appreciated and respected. Even though he desired to gain security from his relationships, he gravitated toward relationship with people who were demanding or frustrated with him. Arnold's past and present become intertwined in his narrative. His stories reflected past memories mixed in with present day situations, revealing unresolved issues. His lack of fluidity and sequence in his storytelling shows an inability to integrate the events of his past.	Debbie, who grew up in a very chaotic and fearful environment, has internalized the chaos and fear. From her mother, who lived with a constant sense of dread and anxiety, Debbie learned the world is not a safe place and something "bad" is going to happen. Due to her mother functioning in a disoriented manner, Debbie has no constancy to build a secure view of her world. Dad was "scary" due to his outbursts of rage and abusiveness, which added to Debbie's internalized belief that the world is unsafe and unreliable. Her parents, a source of comfort, were also a source of danger and fear for her. This left Debbie frozen in a stance between avoidance and approach. She lived from a hypervigilant "on-guard" stance—tracking all fear inducing situations. As life progressed, Debbie struggled with emotional, social, and cognitive difficulties. Her internal disorganization will impair her future interactions with others and inhibit her ability to function well. She will have a poor coping capacity and a marked inability to regulate emotional responses, stay focused, and "on track" in life. Debbie's narrative regarding her childhood was incoherent and at times included long pauses of silence. The interaction itself strongly suggested unresolved traumas. Entire blocks of time from her past could not be accounted for or only remembered in a very disorganized way.

APPENDIX 4
Reset Your Brain's Normal to Joy, Appreciation, and Quiet[1]

1. Fill your Appreciation Memories List with between 5 and 10 Appreciation Memories.

    a. Avoid the splinters of pain that come from memories of people who are no longer with you, whether through death, divorce, moving, job changes, etc. We want 10 "clean" Appreciation Memories. (As you begin, it may be challenging to find pain-free memories. Using memories of very brief moments of appreciation can be helpful—thinking of my favorite sweater or a delicious cup of coffee both work well for me.)

    I recommend that at least two of these be memories involving nature or pets. These memories are more likely to be splinter-free and helpful in restoring our relational circuits and appreciation at those times when people seem like a problem to solve.

2. Once you have 5 to 10 Appreciation Memories on your list, this is your 9-minute exercise:

    a. Take 2 minutes to do the Shalom My Body exercises to restore your relational circuits.

    b. Take 5 minutes to focus on your Appreciation Memories, one at a time. Set a timer so you can concentrate on your memories.

        i. Choose one memory to begin, and fully enter into that memory, remembering how you felt in your body and emotions, and what you saw, heard, smelled, tasted, and touched at the time.

        ii. Remain in this memory until the sense of "being there" begins to fade. Memories are like chewing gum—they can lose their flavor after chewing!

        iii. When the flavor of the memory fades, move to another memory on your list. Again, fully enter in. Continue to do this until the 5 minutes are over.

---

1 | Based on the work of Jim Wilder, Life Model Works.

3. After your 5-minute Memory Visit, take 2 minutes for Simple Quiet with Deep Breathing. Breathe in through your nose and out through pursed lips. Allow your diaphragm to expand.

4. Repeat this 9-minute exercise 3 times a day, and within 30 days, your brain will be rewired to notice things to appreciate in your environment, and you'll begin to find it easier to quiet yourself in moments of anxiety, upset, or other stress.

APPENDIX 5
Immanuel Journaling

Dear God, I am thankful for...

From this point forward, write as if God is talking to you:

My dear child...

I can see you...

I can hear you...

**I understand how big this is for you, how you feel.
I value you.**

I understand how...

**I am glad to be with you. I view your weakness
tenderly.**

I am glad to be with you. I...

**I CAN DO SOMETHING ABOUT WHAT YOU ARE
GOING THROUGH.**

I can do something with you and for you...

Read your results aloud, preferably to another person.

APPENDIX 6
Changing Motivation From Fear to Love[1]

Our direction and goals come from our thoughts. Our motivation comes from our emotions. While we work very hard to educate our thoughts and correct our beliefs, few people train or perfect their motivation with equal discipline. As far as our nervous systems are concerned, our minds run well when motivated by love and desire and poorly when motivated by fear. From a moral point of view, love is also superior. Perfect, that is to say, mature *teleios* love casts out fear. (1 John 4:18)

It should not come as a surprise that fear motives creep into our lives as we fail to mature properly. We learn our motivation during infancy through bonded relationships. Whatever emotions our parents use to motivate us become our internal source of motivation during life. If these early bonds form from love and closeness they serve us well but if they form from fear and the avoidance of pain our motivational system stays immature.

Fear bonds form as the result of failed attempts at self-preservation. While self-preservation is the great value of fear, early experiences in fearful relationships we cannot escape, produce very negative and upsetting internal emotions. When these unpleasant emotions exceed our capacity to return to joy and quiet on our own, we begin to avoid pain as a form of self-preservation. After a while, avoiding pain becomes the central focus of fear bonds even when there is no real risk of overwhelming our capacity.

Once avoiding pain becomes the goal we hear phrases like, "What if he gets mad?" "Are you going to be upset?" "I'm afraid that—fill in the blank" "I'd be too embarrassed!" "You are really pissing me off!" "I have to make him/it stop." I can't stand it when..." "What difference will it make?"

We must then ask a serious question about avoiding pain and overwhelming feelings. Is it self-preservation if I stop being and acting like myself? When I no longer do or say or act like what I really feel inside, isn't my "self" lost? When I can no longer even figure out what I want, feel or even think, haven't I lost my "self" already?

---

1 | © E. James Wilder 2004, This handout is available online at www.lifemodel.org/download/Changing%20Fear%20to%20Love.pdf

What we discover in many people who are fear-bonded and motivated is a loss and obscuring of personal feelings, thoughts, values and desires. They are afraid to make an impact on others. Often the fear is that they will not have an impact or make a difference. Fear bonded people are also quite confused about what fears are theirs and which ones belong to others. Just being around anxious people makes them edgy or distressed. They often withdraw, placate, entertain or please others to make the fear stop. Often the result is that they take on responsibilities that are not theirs because they are afraid of what will happen if they don't. Other times they shrink back from their duties because they feel inadequate.

Another group of fear-bonded individuals are afraid to let others have an impact because they fear losing their own impact. These controllers frequently control people around them with anger, contempt, rejection, ridicule, the "silent treatment," and other ways of creating pain including physical violence.

Naturally we recognize these behaviors as representing brains that have lost their synchronization at level 2. They are operating out of fear and a desire to make things stop instead of synchronizing with others (level 3) or expressing their own values, goals, desires and preferences (level 4.) They have lost their flavor. They have ceased to be lights. Thinking they are preserving themselves they have lost themselves and disappeared.

Before we can understand how to change a fear-bond back to a desire/love-bond, let us review how a healthy identity would deal with fears at each level of development. From this review we can see where we need to start correcting the fear-bond.

Avoiding Fear-Bonds at Each Level of Maturity

1. **Infant maturity**
   a. Recognize the fear (what am I really afraid of?).
   b. Know who I want with me when I am afraid.
   c. Discover what I want (desire).
   d. Talk about my fear.

2. **Child Maturity**
   a. Recognize my part in the fearful situation.
   b. Recognize the other person's part in the fearful situation.
   c. Use a third person to check my reality.
   d. Separate my responsibility from yours (a+b).
   e. Learn to be myself rather than control others.

3. **Adult**
   a. Stay in relationship while letting others have fears.
   b. Do nothing about what others fear—let them handle it.
   c. Take care of our own business with personal style.
   d. Remind self and others about our mutual goals and desires.

There is a big separation between adult and higher levels of maturity when it comes to handling fears. Up to this point every person is responsible for their own fears and no one else's. Without many years of practice distinguishing *this fear is mine* from *that fear is yours*, then moving to higher levels of dealing with fear will only bring confusion about responsibility. The shift of responsibility from dealing with my own fears to helping others with their fears is a major sign of dysfunction when it is attempted by anyone of adult maturity or lower. Even for parents, taking on the fears of others is dysfunctional outside the parent/child relationship.

Parents must be very careful not to develop fear-bonds in their children. Since parents want to build capacity in their children, they help children back to joy from fear and teach them to act like themselves during manageable levels of the emotion.

4. **Parent**
   a. Help one's personal people (natural and spiritual family).
   b. Take some shared responsibility for the fears of younger minds.
   c. Identify fears in the younger mind.
   d. Help the younger mind return to joy and peace.

5. **Elder**
   a. Help "at risk," isolated, marginalized people.
   b. Identify community fears.
   c. Help community remember what is like us to do.
   d. Remain a non-anxious presence.

Elders, as we know, act like parents-at-large for their communities. Elders will provide just barely enough security for people to recognize and face their own fears knowing that they are not alone and remembering what is really important to "our people" under these scary conditions.

Converting Fear to Desire Based On Our Maturity Level

Now, the reason for our discussion was to change fear-bonds to love-bonds where our desires and identity can shine. To make a change from fear to love we start first with the adult level. If we can correct the problem at this level it will be easiest. The adult will simply think and decide differently, and the problem is solved.

SOLUTIONS:

1. Confidently be yourself. Take care of your business. Stay in relationship with others around you who are anxious but do nothing about their part of the problem. Speak of mutual goals that are important during this time of threat and fear.

    If this adult solution worked, then you have corrected the fear bond. This does not mean that others will not react by trying to put pressure on you to become frightened again, so you may have to make this correction several times under even more pressure and anxiety from others.

    If you still feel fear or cannot imagine how to use an adult solution we must go deeper and correct some earlier problems that lead to fear bonds. First we look at the child level skills. Resolving fear-bonds at the child level is not just a matter of understanding and choosing differently. These solutions take longer and involve study and consultation with others. They require a good deal of problem solving to figure out "mine" from "yours." We generally do not solve these problems without consultation and encouragement.

2. Define your responsibilities carefully. Go through the demands you feel you must meet and see which ones are logically yours and which are unreasonable. Find someone qualified to double-check your judgment. Now, be equally clear when you are trying to solve someone else's problem or fear. You should now be able to speak clearly about what is yours and what is someone else's part of the problem and solution.

3. Check to see if someone else is controlling you by being upset or threatening to become upset. If you are being controlled return to step 2 until you can speak calmly and clearly to them about your responsibilities and boundaries.

4. Check and see if you are attempting to control others through your threats or upset. If so return to step 2 until you can speak calmly and clearly to them about your responsibilities and boundaries.

If you still fear and cannot imagine or manage to speak clearly to others about your responsibilities and limits, then we must go deeper and correct problems and develop skills needed for the infant level. We get here when we can't figure things out on our own or even if we do, the fear is strong enough that we can't talk freely and openly about who we are, so our "self" continues to be hidden and lost when we are afraid.

5. Find out what I am really afraid of with help from experienced minds. Often what I am afraid of is not a current day reality or what it seems to me. I may think I am afraid I am not doing my job but I am really afraid someone will be angry or ridicule me. I am afraid I will not survive being ridiculed because of my early life experiences.

6. I must discover who I want with me when I am afraid and what I want them to do with or for me. I need someone who can handle the fear without being overwhelmed and help me focus on myself instead of the threat I perceive.

7. I must discover what I really want and what really matters most to me in the current situation so that I can express my goals and values.

8. I must learn to speak about what matters to me even while I feel afraid by having someone patiently help me find words I can mean and practice saying them in a low threat situation until I am ready to speak of my values, goals and preferences to others who are afraid or of whom I am afraid.

This process of defining and expressing our identities gets much easier as our identities mature and become solid. The farther we have grown, the easier it is to change fear-bonds to love-bonds.

APPENDIX 7
Types A + B Traumas

TYPE A AND TYPE B TRAUMAS	
TYPE A TRAUMAS	**TYPE B TRAUMAS**
Type A trauma is harmful by its *absence*, which causes damage to our emotions. To some degree, one or more of Type A traumas will typically be found in each stage of our lives, and we can all find at least one Type A trauma wound that needs attention. When you look at the Maturity Indicators Chart, you will see that a failure by the Family and Community—the middle column—produces a Type A trauma. In fact, *absences* in those areas define what Type A traumas are. Here are a few *absences* that illustrate Type A traumas:	Type B trauma is harmful by its *presence*. Having been on the receiving end of the following experiences can create a Type B trauma. There is a range of severity in Type B traumas. It is important to remember that to discount "lesser" traumas is to avoid the truth about how much it hurts, and thereby miss the chance for healing. Avoiding or ignoring wounds does not make them go away. Here are some harmful events that are examples of Type B traumas:
1. Being cherished and celebrated by one's parents simply by virtue of one's existence.	1. Physical abuse, including face slapping, hair pulling, shaking, punching, and tickling a child into hysteria.
2. Having the experience of being a delight.	2. Any spanking which becomes violent, leaving marks or bruises or emotional scars.
3. Having a parent take the time to understand who you are—encouraging you to share who you are, what you think, and what you feel.	3. Sexual abuse including inappropriate touching, sexual kissing or hugging, intercourse, oral or anal sex, voyeurism, exhibitionism, or the sharing of the parent's sexual experiences with a child.
4. Receiving large amounts of non-sexual physical nurturing—laps to sit in, arms to hold, and a willingness to let you go when you have had enough.	4. Verbal abuse or name-calling.

5. Being given age-appropriate limits. Having those limits enforced in ways that do not call your value into question.	5. Abandonment by a parent.
6. Being given adequate food, clothing, shelter, medical, and dental care.	6. Torture or satanic ritual abuse.
7. Being taught how to do hard things—to problem solve and to develop persistence.	7. Witnessing someone else being abused.
8. Being taught how to develop personal resources and talents.	

APPENDIX 8
S.A.S.H.E.T.
SAD ◊ ANGRY ◊ SCARED ◊ HAPPY ◊ EXCITED ◊ TENDER

CHECKING IN

One essential aspect of building vibrant families of Jesus (true church) is equipping people to connect with one another on the heart level, which allows people to build joy. Joy means glad to be together no matter what. One practice that helps us live out that value is *checking in* using S.A.S.H.E.T.: Sad, Angry, Scared, Happy, Excited, Tender. We practice sharing how we are feeling in almost all of our gatherings. From our daily interactions, to our families gathered around dinner tables, to our weekly small group or simple church meetings, we check in. Even in our leadership meetings, we have found that with a simple check in round, our hearts are connected and we become more relational even through difficult discussions.

SAD

Low Energy, beaten down, exhausted, tired, weak, listless, depressed, detached, withdrawn, indifferent, apathetic, lazy, bored

Sad, unhappy, crushed, dejected, depressed, desperate, hopeless, grieved, heavy, despairing, weepy

Betrayed, deceived, mortified, humiliated, disillusioned, distrustful

Ashamed, guilty, mortified, humiliated, embarrassed, exposed, stupid

Disappointed, let down, disheartened, disillusioned, distrustful

Invisible, forgotten, overlooked, unimportant, invisible, disregarded, lost

Despised, ridiculed, dumb, belittled, mocked, scorned, shamed, hated, detested

ANGRY

Angry, annoyed, controlled, manipulated, furious, grouchy, grumpy, irritated, provoked, frustrated, hateful, cold, icy, bitter, cynical

SCARED

Anxious, afraid, uneasy, nauseated, nervous, restless, preoccupied, worried, scared, tense, fearful, terrified, insecure, indecisive, hyper-vigilant, cautious

Overwhelmed, apprehensive, boxed in, burdened, confused, distressed, guarded, hard-pressed, paralyzed, panicky, tense, weighted down, edgy

Traumatized, shocked, disturbed, injured, damaged, unloved, hated

Confused, baffled, perplexed, mystified, bewildered, misunderstood, disoriented

HAPPY

Happy, cheerful, delighted, elated, encouraged, glad, gratified, joyful, lightheared, overjoyed, pleased, relieved, satisfied, thrilled, secure, optimistic

Confident, positive, secure, self-assured, assertive

Peaceful, relieved, at ease, calm, comforted, cool, relaxed, composed, protected

EXCITED

High Energy, energetic, enthusiastic, excited, playful, rejuvenated, talkative, pumped, motivated, driven, determined, obsessed, jittery

Amazed, stunned, surprised, shocked, jolted, enlightened

TENDER

Loving, affectionate, cozy, passionate, romantic, sexy, warm, tender, responsive, thankful, appreciative, refreshed, pleased, comforted, reassured

Alone, avoidant, lonely, abandoned, deserted, isolated, cut off, detached, disconnected, unwanted

GO DEEPER
Further Resources

BOOKS

- *Attune to Attach*, Maribeth Poole, (Attachment Styles)
- *Building Bounce*, Marcus Warner, Stefanie Hinman (Emotional resilience)
- *40 Nuggets for Life*, Barbara Moon (Life Model exercises)
- *The 4 Habits of Joy-Filled Marriages*, Chris Coursey, Marcus Warner (Marriage, Relationships)
- *How We Love*, Milan and Kay Yerkovich (Attachment Styles)
- *Joy-Filled Relationships*, Barbara Moon (Relationships, Life Model)
- *Joyful Journey*, E. James Wilder, John and Sungshim Loppnow, Anna Kang (Immanuel Journaling)
- *Joy Starts Here*, E. James Wilder, Chris Coursey, Ed Khouri, Shelia Sutton (Joy, Protector)
- *The Joy Switch*, Chris Coursey (Relational Circuit)
- *Living from the Heart Jesus Gave You*, Jim Wilder, James Friesen, Maribeth Poole, Anne Bierling (Life Model, Maturity)
- *Other Half of Church*, Michel Hendricks, E. James Wilder, (Whole-brained Christianity)
- *Outsmarting Yourself*, Dr. Karl Lehman (Relational Circuit, Triggering)
- *The Pandora Problem*, E. James Wilder (Group Identity, Narcissism)
- *The Pandora Problem Companion Guide*, Barbara Moon (Group Identity, Narcissism)
- *Rare Leadership*, Marcus Warner, Jim Wilder, (Leadership, Maturity)
- *REAL Prayer*, Marcus Warner (Healing, Connection)
- *Re-Framing Your Hurts*, Barbara Moon (Relationships, Healing)
- *Relational Skills in the Bible*, Amy Brown, Chris Coursey (Bible study, Relational Brain Skills)
- *Share Immanuel*, E. James Wilder, Chris Coursey (Healing, Connection)
- *Slaying the Monster*, Marcus Warner (Healing)
- *The Solution of Choice*, Marcus Warner, E. James Wilder (Transformation)

- *30 Days of Joy*, Chris and Jen Coursey (Marriage)
- *Transforming Fellowship*, Chris Coursey (Relational Brain Skills)
- *Transitions to Transformation*, Maribeth Poole, (Maturity Stages)
- *Understanding the Wounded Heart*, Marcus Warner (Emotional Healing)
- *What Every Believer Should Know About Spiritual Warfare*, Marcus Warner (Spiritual Warfare)
- *The Whole-Brained Child*, Dr. Daniel Siegel (Brain skills and children)

VIDEO AND OTHER

- Online Practice Community, Amy Brown, THRIVEtoday.org, (Monthly and recorded relational skills training)
- E-Institute + Online Conferences, deeperwalkinternational.org
- Online Groups, lifemodelworks.org
- Joy Streams, lifemodelworks.org
- The Path, deeperwalkinternational.org
- YouTube.com
  - Deeper Walk International
  - THRIVEtoday (Chris Coursey)
  - Life Model Works
  - Presence and Practice
  - Dedicated Web Design (Maribeth Poole)
- Blogs:
  - www.thrivingmamas.org
  - www.presenceandpractice.com/blog
  - www.lifemodelworks.org/blog
  - www.barbaramoonbooks.com/index.php/barbara-moon-author-speaker

AMY HAMILTON BROWN

Amy Hamilton Brown is a content developer, author, trainer, and visionary. Some years ago, she found herself being transformed by the relational concepts of joy, appreciation, interactive connection with God, and heart-focused community. Over time, she began to envision small groups that could gather around these ideas, build friendships, and connect deeply with God. Out of that vision, Journey Groups were born.

Amy is a content developer, trainer, and consultant on staff with Alive & Well, Inc. As consultant, she creates monthly training events for the Online Practice Community with THRIVEtoday, creates training materials for Life Model Works, and leads the Certified Journey Group Leadership Community with Deeper Walk International. She co-authored the book *Relational Skills in the Bible* with Chris Coursey, and she is a relational skills trainer with THRIVEtoday.

Prior to working with Alive & Well, Deeper Walk, and THRIVEtoday, Amy worked as a paralegal and led recovery groups with a focus on building connection with God and others. She is an ordained minister through her home congregation, Gadsden Vineyard Church.

ACKNOWLEDGEMENTS

Where do I begin? Journey Groups would not have been born without the encouragement and practices of Toni Daniels at Lk10.com, nor would it have continued and been written without Misa Garavaglia and Sue Sather as my early partners in this venture. Those who joined me in the early versions of Journey Groups in 2016 and 2017, you know who you are, and you are dear to me.

Thank you to every one of the Journey Group Leaders who has walked through these materials with our wonderful members. You've prayed, taught, and loved well.

None of these transformational concepts are mine. I stand on the shoulders of many men and women who identified, developed, and applied the concepts—Dr. Jim Wilder, Kitty Wilder, Chris and Jen Coursey, Ed and Maritza Khouri, Maribeth Poole, Anne Bierling, Shelia Sutton, Dr. Karl Lehman, Charlotte Lehman, Marcus Warner, John and Sungshim Loppnow, Anna Kang, Margaret Webb, and Jessie Handy Duisberg.

My past and current family at Deeper Walk International is amazing—Marcus and Brenda Warner, Nik Harrang, Kimberly Rigsby, Stephanie Warner, Erin Kowall, Kristine Bassett, Timothy Jensen, and Bibi Taylor. If you can imagine staff meetings full of laughter, love, and prayer, you can imagine this team. Many thanks to every one of you, especially the secret weapons for Journey Groups—Erin and Kristine, and my incredible editor, Stephanie Warner. (Huzzah!) So much love for this bunch.

Chris and Jen Coursey at THRIVEtoday believed in me before I did, and I love and thank you for your encouragement. And those boys!

Margaret and Jerry Webb, lots of fun times to come in the Ozarks. Love!

Livy, Brian, Bruce, Ellen, Randy, and Chris—thank you for providing a home for this gypsy! Adam, Erin, Livy, and Che—you made me a mom and have forever made me proud. Thank you for learning from my mistakes. I love you all.

Deeper Walk International is a 501(C)(3) nonprofit bringing together biblically-balanced teaching on emotional healing and spiritual warfare that helps people who feel stuck break through to new levels of freedom in their walk with God.

We teach about God's grace, life in the Spirit, spiritual warfare, and authentic community. What sets our training apart is how we bring it all together, then make it simple and transferable, so that people understand what it takes to walk in freedom and grow in maturity.

We call this approach to ministry "heart-focused discipleship."

Find us at DeeperWalkInternational.org.

the world wounds us

the devil lies to us

we vow never to let it happen again

we spend our lives picking the fruit of our wounds

It doesn't have to stay this way.

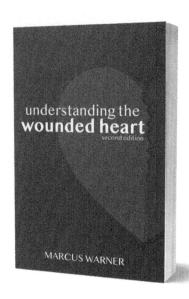

Life is hard.

We all get overwhelmed at times.

But some people seem to bounce back from their upset emotions faster than most.

Are they just born happy?

Or is there **a secret to building emotional resilience that anyone can learn**?

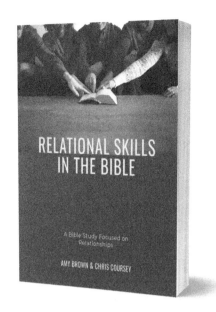

Journey into the pages of Scripture to see relationships as never before!

This fun, flexible, eye-opening Bible study focuses attention on what matters most in life: relationships!

There is Hope for narcissists.

Are you ready to open the box?

Most of us are scared to death to lift the lid on the Pandora's box of narcissism. Dealing with predatory people leaves us intimidated, scared, and hopeless.

Find a clear view of both the problem and the surprising solution.

Flesh-filled homes breed conflict and pain.

Spirit-filled homes grow the maturity to handle hard things in loving ways.

Participation in the battle is not optional.

We are all in this war whether we like it or not, so *doesn't it make sense to be prepared?*

These and other resources can be found at
www.DeeperWalkInternational.org

Made in the USA
Monee, IL
12 August 2021